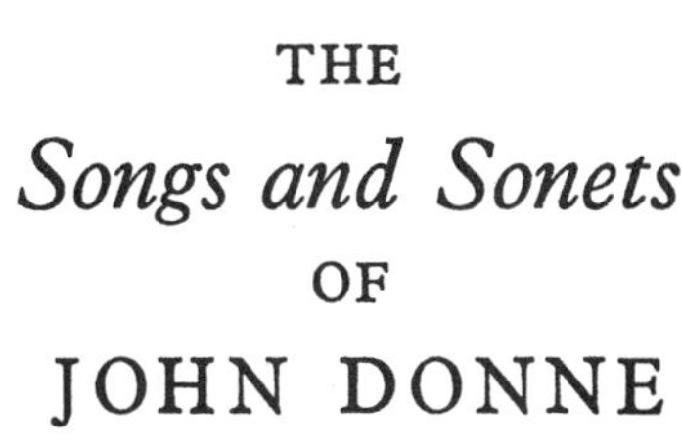

THE *Songs and Sonets* OF JOHN DONNE

An *Editio minor* with
Introduction and Explanatory Notes by

THEODORE REDPATH

*Fellow of Trinity College, Cambridge
and Lecturer in English in the
University of Cambridge*

METHUEN AND CO. LTD

11 NEW FETTER LANE · LONDON EC4

First published 1956

First published as a University Paperback 1967
Reprinted five times
Reprinted 1979

ISBN 0 416 69660 0

Printed in Great Britain at the
University Press, Cambridge

I dedicate this little edition to my Mother and to the memory of my Father.

T. R.

PREFACE

THE present volume has a twofold origin. It arises partly out of my academic work and partly out of a personal experience.

In the course of supervising Cambridge undergraduates for honours degrees in English, I have become convinced that the men require an edition of Donne's *Songs and Sonets*, containing notes on every point likely to cause difficulty to a reader of reasonable intelligence. Such an edition has not previously appeared, nor do the notes in any edition of the Poetical Works, or in any selection, hitherto published, fulfil this requirement. Even the notes in Professor Grierson's epoch-making edition of Donne's Poetical Works do not meet the precise case, quite apart from the bulk of those volumes, and the expense of purchasing them. Professor Grierson's purpose was clearly quite different from the present purpose, for which a far greater *number* of notes are required than appear in his edition; but for which, on the other hand, many of his notes are fuller than is necessary.

The other source of the present volume was the visit to Cambridge a few winters ago of a friend of the family, to whom Donne was hitherto entirely unknown, and to whom I read some of the *Songs and Sonets*, by way of a friendly exchange for having some Spanish and German poems read to me. Our friend was enchanted with the *Songs and Sonets*, but often only after considerable explanation. This made me think that there was probably a place for an edition for the general reader, which would bring these remarkable poems to readers both in England and abroad, neither merely as a sometimes exasperatingly obscure plain text, nor as part of a bulky specialist volume or series of volumes.

It seemed to me on further consideration that my university purpose and this more general purpose could be combined, at the comparatively small cost of probably irritating some readers by including notes on points which they might regard as obvious, and of perplexing others (and perhaps some of the same readers) by including certain references to variant readings, which might at first sight be thought to be of interest only to scholars. On the former point I

have been considerably influenced by the revelations of that unique book, *Practical Criticism* by Professor I. A. Richards, which makes it amply clear that even considerable numbers of English students of poetry, at universities where the standard of education is certainly high, make elementary blunders in disentangling even the literal sense of poetry less elusive than much to be found in the *Songs and Sonets*. With regard to variants, I have found, in the course of reading Donne with students, that, in many cases, a consideration of variants has strikingly sharpened our impression of the passages concerned.

A great problem for me has been to what lengths I should go in interpretation; what amount of interpretation I should, in this particular case, take editing to involve. In the end I have adhered to the practice of not attempting full interpretations of the poems, and contented myself with hinting, in a few particularly interesting cases, at a full realization of the poems concerned. The edition therefore leaves readers plenty of scope for interpretation of the poems, though, on the other hand, I should hold that interpretations which contradict undoubted meanings, such as many of those to which attention has been drawn in these notes, must of necessity be wrong. Again, even on particular points, I have preferred to err, if at all, by not indulging in a chase for ambiguities and recherché interpretations; not because I dislike ingenuity, but because I have here set myself only the more modest task of clearing the ground.

In compiling the notes I have drawn, where I thought it advisable, on the work of previous editors, my obligations to whom are acknowledged in the appropriate places. My greatest debt is to the work of Professor Sir Herbert Grierson, without which so many of us might well have known little of Donne. Professor Grierson's notes, which have thrown light on so many dark places, need no praise of mine: but, as a subsequent editor, I owe my gratitude to them. Where I have differed from Grierson, either on interpretation or on the text, it has always been with a sense of respect.

In addition to writing the notes, I have also completely revised the text, largely on the basis of the variants noted by Grierson,[1] but also taking account of certain of the manuscript evidence which has come to light since his great edition was published. My revi-

1. The present edition therefore makes no pretensions to being textually an *editio major*: though I have re-examined a number of the MSS.

sion of the text has not resulted in much departure from Grierson's. With respect to the canon I have followed him completely. With regard to the text of individual poems I have departed from him on occasion. Wherever I have done so, on any point of sufficient importance, I have explained my reasons for doing so, in the notes. I had originally intended adding textual notes, to cover *all* my departures from Grierson's text, but after taking Sir Herbert's own opinion on the point, I have decided not to burden the work with a large critical apparatus.

Except where there was some very special reason for not doing so, I have everywhere modernized the spelling. To the bibliopurist this may appear a retrograde step, but for my present purpose, where an understanding of the poems is the paramount object, any quaintness of impression, so easily produced by the sight of Elizabethan or Jacobean spelling, is to be carefully avoided. A minor problem arising from this, has been whether to retain initial capitals. I have decided only to retain these where to do so seems to contribute to an understanding of the poem, despite the somewhat unfamiliar impression they are likely to make.

The matter of punctuation has been fascinating, but at times almost unendurably teasing. Professor Grierson's purpose and my own are quite distinct on this point. Grierson was concerned to establish an accurate text, in the old spelling, and in a punctuation which would probably have been Donne's, had the poet himself revised the text of his poems for the press. My own purpose, on the other hand, has been to produce a text in modern spelling, and in a punctuation designed to aid in bringing out to a modern reader (whether a silent reader or a reader reading aloud), the full meaning of the poem concerned. I have found, as I have gone through the poems, that the Elizabethan, Jacobean, or Caroline punctuation often does this, but sometimes has the opposite effect. I have in every case tested the point by my general principle, and adopted the punctuation which passed the test. The variations of punctuation from Grierson's text, with a defence of my departures where these seemed of sufficient importance, would have appeared in the textual notes, but since I have decided to dispense with textual notes, I have included the most important cases in the general notes. With regard to the old editions, one common case of difference between my text and that of the 1633 edition (to take the most important edition) is in the matter of commas. Very often, admittedly, the comma at the end of a line in the 1633 edition, where we might expect a semi-colon, is correct, even according to my principle, since it expresses a hurrying-on of the sense, which is typical of Donne. Sometimes, on the other hand, no such hurrying-on seems to occur, and yet there is a mere comma in the 1633 edition. In such cases, it has seemed to me, the explanation is probably that the comma had different limits of value in sixteenth- and seventeenth-century English from those which it has today, and I have therefore often used a semi-colon in such cases, or even, where a still longer stop seemed to be required, a full colon. I hope that those who, in my view, are too puristically inclined on this point, will give due weight to the consideration that a poem does not maintain its life constantly in any one set of marks on paper, but that at different periods the same poem, with all its subtlety of intonation, may be correctly represented by different sets of signs, and, in particular, by different marks of punctuation: that, in the present case, what one must try to be faithful to, when producing a modern text, is Donne's finesse, passion, argumentary evolution, and rhythmic spirit, and that, *where one has to choose*, it is far worse to be unfaithful to these than to a mere system of signs, which often exhibits nothing but a creaking antiquity without any of its original functional life. Those who may feel inclined to object to the policy I have adopted may cease to do so if they bear in mind the ascertainable fact that the punctuation of even the best extant manuscripts is often very different from that of the early printed editions, and so realize the possibility that those editions may often owe their punctuation to editors or printers and not to Donne's own intentions.

It is appropriate to end this Preface by expressing acknowledgement for help received. My first debt of gratitude is to Professor Sir Herbert Grierson himself, who very kindly read through most of my typescript at an early stage, and discussed doubtful points with me at some length on several occasions. On points of detail he has made a number of highly useful suggestions, and he has also given me the benefit of his wise advice on matters of policy. I was indeed fortunate to have guidance from one who is, in this realm, so obviously *facile princeps*. My second obligation is to Professor Basil Willey, Fellow of Pembroke College, and King Edward VII Professor of English Literature in the University of Cambridge, for his encouragement, advice and help to me soon after I had set out on this project. Two of my most recent debts are to Mr F. L. Lucas, Fellow of King's College, and Reader in English in the University of Cambridge, and Mr T. R. Henn, Fellow and Senior Tutor of St Catharine's College, and Lecturer in English in the University of Cambridge, who have given their valuable time in reading through my typescript in its almost final form, and made most useful criticisms and suggestions. I owe thanks also to Sir Geoffrey Keynes for kindly letting me work on the Leconfield and Luttrell manuscripts: and similar thanks to the Rev. W. M. Atkins, Librarian of St Paul's Cathedral Library, for permission to work on the St Paul's manuscript. Finally, I wish to say how grateful I am to Mr W. G. Ingram, Lecturer in Education in the University of Cambridge, whose immense help, throughout the period of proof-reading and final revision, has greatly benefited the edition, and has made this last stage not only bearable but enjoyable.

THEODORE REDPATH

Trinity College
Cambridge
June 1955

NOTE ON THE SECOND IMPRESSION

I have been asked to confine changes to a minimum, and those made are therefore mainly verbal. There are, however, a few alterations and additions of substance. I have benefited from the recent publication of Sir Geoffrey Keynes's *Bibliography of Dr John Donne*, Cambridge, 1958. A few changes are also due to a reading of Professor Pierre Legouis's edition of Selected Poems of Donne (Donne, *Poèmes choisis*, Traduction, introduction et notes par P. Legouis, Paris, n.d. [1955]), and of his article 'Donne, l'amour et les critiques', *Études anglaises*, avril-juin, 1957. Some interesting textual suggestions by Mr John Sparrow (*TLS*, 21 Dec. 1956) have prompted two notes. I also am indebted to Mr G. P. Simons, of the University College of North Staffordshire, for drawing my attention to a possible biblical reference in l. 24 of *The Curse*.

In the above-mentioned letter Mr Sparrow also urges that the canon of the *Songs and Sonets* should include *Elegy X: The Dream.* He rightly indicates that this poem has a quite different rhyme-scheme from all the other Elegies, which are in rhymed couplets. He also points out that the transfer would have the authority of one group of MSS. Mr Sparrow's case seems to me strong; and had I not to restrict changes to a minimum I should have printed the poem with notes. This would, however, have involved many consequential changes, and I must therefore postpone doing so.

January 1959 T. R.

CONTENTS

INTRODUCTION

I. THE STATUS OF THE 'SONGS AND SONETS' IN ENGLISH POETRY

DONNE'S *Songs and Sonets* are among the three or four finest collections of love-lyrics in the English language. Such a high valuation still requires emphasis, despite the fact that these poems are read and appreciated far more than they were, say, fifty years ago. Too many readers of poetry, even in England, would still omit Donne's name from a list of the supreme love-lyrists of England, while readily including the names of Herrick, Shelley, Tennyson, Browning, and Swinburne. This is probably partly because the *Songs and Sonets* still remain comparatively little known:[1] but there are other reasons. One reason is the lingering prejudice that love-lyrics should be expressions of feeling unalloyed with any marked degree of cerebration. Donne's love-lyrics spring partly from a strong and ingenious head. They are therefore liable to give the impression of being merely brain-spun. In fact, that is very seldom the case, since they also come from a passionate heart. Another reason is that many people are put off by the sheer difficulty of the sense of many passages. Ben Jonson prophesied that the poetry of Donne would perish for lack of being understood. It has not yet perished, but though it is read now perhaps much more than at any time since the seventeenth century, it offers much difficulty, and it is doubtful how far even the bare sense of some of the poems is really understood. In the case of the *Songs and Sonets*, however, trouble taken in trying to understand the sense is almost always amply rewarded. A further obstacle to the just evaluation of the poems is the fairly widespread conception of Donne as a merely flippant, cynical love poet. Among the causes of the spread of this

1. In a widely circulated anthology (*The Oxford Book of English Verse*) only 7 pages are allotted to Donne (as compared with 21 to Herrick, 19 to Shelley, 23 to Tennyson, 20 to Browning, and 12 to Swinburne). Moreover, of the seven poems ascribed to Donne, one is probably not by him at all; and only four of the *Songs and Sonets* are given. Again, in the last edition of Palgrave's *Golden Treasury* (1941, reprinted 1954), not a single poem by Donne is included.

idea are probably the choice of cynical poems for anthologies, e.g. the *Song*, 'Go and catch a falling star'; the cumulative impression of the *Songs and Sonets* and the mostly cynical *Elegies*, when taken together; and the influence of certain outstanding critical studies.[1] In actual fact, the *Songs and Sonets* cover a very wide range of feeling from flippant cynicism to the most tender and even idealistic love. Finally, many people fail to find in Donne's love-lyrics the music which they demand from such poems. That is a pity, for there is really great variety and subtlety of music in the *Songs and Sonets*, and once it is properly sensed, it can be felt to have attractions at least equal to and sometimes transcending those of music of a more obvious character.

The *Songs and Sonets* are, in fact, superior as a body of love-lyrics to any equivalent number of poems by Herrick, Shelley, Tennyson, Browning, or Swinburne. Indeed, if we survey English poetry from end to end I doubt if we shall find any serious rivals to the *Songs and Sonets*, except the sonnets of Sidney and Shakespeare, and the love-lyrics of Yeats, and, possibly, of Hardy.

II. THE PLACE OF THE 'SONGS AND SONETS' WITHIN DONNE'S WORK

The *Songs and Sonets* were not all written within one short period, but at various times over probably as much as twenty years, and possibly even more. We have no evidence as to when Donne wrote the first of these poems, whichever that was: but it may even have been before 1590. On the other hand, there is evidence which makes it unlikely that he wrote any of the poems after about the middle of 1614; and there is no positive evidence that he wrote any of them after 1612, when he was forty-one.

According to Drummond, Ben Jonson told him that Donne had written all his best pieces before he was twenty-five years old, i.e. before about the middle of 1596, if Donne was really born in August 1571. We must not, however, allow Jonson's statement to mislead us. It was made in 1618, and therefore, in any case, could not apply to such poems as the great *Hymns*, written after that date. More important for our immediate purpose, it is hardly likely that in

1. Such as that by Professor Pierre Legouis, *Donne the Craftsman*, Paris, 1928.

making the statement Jonson was taking into account such fine poems as *A Nocturnal upon St Lucy's Day* or *A Valediction: forbidding mourning*. *A Nocturnal* was pretty certainly written well after 1596, and possibly as late as 1612, or even 1617 (if it refers to the death of his wife). *A Valediction: forbidding mourning* was very probably written in 1612. In any case, Jonson's statement can at most be evidence that *the best poems of Donne which he had seen by 1618* were written before Donne was twenty-five. Moreover, which of the *Songs and Sonets* Jonson had seen by that date is quite uncertain. Only three of these poems are known to have been printed in whole or in part by 1618, and only two more before Donne's death in 1631. Like many of the poems of his contemporaries, they were circulated in manuscript among friends; but it is worth noting that extant manuscript collections of Donne's poems, with any pretensions at completeness, date largely from 1620, two years after Jonson made his generalization. His knowledge of the poems, therefore, may well have been patchy. Besides, there are definite indications that several of the best *Songs and Sonets* in addition to *A Nocturnal* and *A Valediction: forbidding mourning*, were written well after 1596. *The Canonization* and *The Sun Rising*, for instance, were probably written after the accession of James I (1603), while *Twickenham Garden* was almost certainly written after 1608, when Lady Bedford began to occupy Twickenham Park.

There is, on the other hand, as I have said, no positive evidence that any of the *Songs and Sonets* were written after 1612. There is the bare possibility that *A Nocturnal* was written later, but on the whole it seems unlikely. With regard to forty-five out of the fifty-five *Songs and Sonets* accepted and printed by Grierson, it is indeed virtually certain from external evidence that they were written before mid-1614, and of the remaining ten (some of which are comparatively unimportant) only *A Nocturnal* seems the sort of poem which could have been written after that date. Donne took holy orders at the beginning of 1615, and he was already preparing to do so in the latter half of 1614. He took the step extremely seriously, and it is almost out of the question that he should have written any of these poems after he made his final decision.

We may then with a high degree of confidence say that all the

1. For details see Sir Geoffrey Keynes's *Bibliography of Dr John Donne*, Cambridge, 1958.

Songs and Sonets, with the possible though unlikely exception of *A Nocturnal*, were written before the middle of 1614, when Donne was forty-three.

The assignment of individual poems to dates within the long period in which they were all written, is, in our present state of knowledge, impossible with any precision, except in a few cases. On the other hand, it is possible to assign a fair number of them with reasonable probability to earlier or later parts of the period, on internal grounds. Capital dates are 1598, when Donne first met Anne More, his future wife, and December 1601, when he married her. A considerable number of the poems, including some of the more flippantly cynical ones, such as *The Indifferent* and the *Song*, 'Go and catch a falling star', were probably written before Donne met Anne More in 1598, and were therefore probably contemporary with most of the *Elegies* and *Satires*. Other poems express or imply satisfaction, sometimes predominantly physical, sometimes predominantly spiritual, in a relationship of such apparent depth and stability that it may very well have been his marriage and the liaison which led up to it. Such poems, then, were probably written between 1598 and 1614. They include *The Anniversary*, *The Sun Rising*, *A Valediction: of weeping*, and *A Valediction: forbidding mourning*, which last poem, if we may believe Walton's testimony, Donne did definitely write to his wife. Not all the *Songs and Sonets* of this second period, however, were written by Donne to his wife. At least one was written to the Countess of Bedford, and at least one was probably written to Mrs Herbert, though this second case is the subject of some controversy.[1] This period of writing largely coincides with the earlier and larger part of his religious poetry. The date of *The Progress of the Soul*, for instance, which, though indeed a satire, is also a religious poem, is 1601: and reliable authorities hold that the majority of the other religious poems were written between 1607 and 1614. It is therefore a complete mistake to think of Donne as renouncing secular poetry for religious poetry at the time of his ordination. To realize the true situation helps one to understand a particularly interesting feature of the *Songs and Sonets* of this second period, namely that so many of them are shot

1. See, for instance, Professor Garrod's article 'Donne and Mrs Herbert' (in *RES*, July 1945), and Mr J. B. Leishman's *The Monarch of Wit*, Hutchinson, London, 1951.

through with religious references and suggestions. Donne himself, in one of the *Holy Sonnets*, even asserts a causal connection between his love for his wife, and his increasing concern for religion:

> Here the admiring her my mind did whet
> To seek thee, God; so streams do shew the head.

This concern came in turn to pervade the love poetry of this second period, not only that probably written to his wife, but also that certainly or probably written to other women.

After his ordination Donne wrote little poetry of any sort. He forsook poetry for his religious duties, for prayers and for sermons, those wonderful sermons which some discriminating critics have rated as high as his poetry.

Let us now look a little more closely at Donne's other activities during the two periods in which the *Songs and Sonets* were written.

During the first period (*c.* 1590–8) Donne was first at Cambridge (1587–90), where he came after a corresponding period at Oxford; then in London as a law student and a 'great visitor of ladies' and 'frequenter' of the theatre (1591–4); later, on his travels in Italy and Spain (?1595–6); and still later, on board one of Essex's men-of-war in the expeditions against Cadiz (1596) and to the Azores (1597). To this period belong the first four of Donne's five unwieldy but quite witty *Satires* (*c.* 1593–7), plentiful in ripe speech about the life and abuses of the London of the day, but plentiful also in the marks of study and learning. These satires bear strong traces of the influence both of Horace and of Persius. To the same period belong the *Epigrams*, moderately dexterous 'imitations' of Martial. More important, most of the *Elegies* belong to this period. Here we have love poems under the direct impact of Ovid.[1] All this work thus bears marks of strong influences. No scholar has so far discovered any correspondingly strong influence on the *Songs and Sonets*. That may be a token of essential originality. Towards the end of the same period (1597 onwards) Donne began writing verse-letters to his contemporaries. Among the first are the two letters probably written to his friend Christopher Brooke, called *The Storm* and *The Calm*, describing the great storm in June 1597, which wrecked the

1. The influence of Ovid on Donne's *Elegies* is well treated by Mr J. B. Leishman in *The Monarch of Wit*.

large fleet Elizabeth had fitted out to destroy a second armada which was being prepared by the King of Spain. These poems show Donne's remarkable talent for descriptive poetry. Donne's only extant prose works of this period are most of the *Paradoxes and Problems*, a few miscellaneous essays, and the early *Letters*. The *Paradoxes and Problems* and the essays are written in a tone of lively flippancy, and they are full of ingenious sallies and striking comparisons. The *Letters* are also always lively and sometimes witty, besides being of biographical interest. In both the verse and the prose we find from time to time thoughts or images which also occur in the *Songs and Sonets*: but, with the exception of one or two of the *Elegies* and *Verse-Letters*, Donne created no work of art comparable in quality with the *Songs and Sonets*.

Let us now turn to the second period (1598–1614). In 1598 Donne was appointed private secretary to Sir Thomas Egerton, Lord Keeper of the Great Seal. He had served with Egerton's son in the Cadiz expedition. Egerton *père* was evidently struck by Donne's 'learning, languages and other ability'. Donne seems to have worked hard and well for Egerton until 1601,[1] when he was dismissed for having secretly married Anne More, niece of Egerton's second wife. At the instigation of Sir George More, Anne's father, Donne was even imprisoned in the Fleet (February 1602). After his release later in the year, Donne, whose promising career was now blasted, lived for some years on charity and patronage. He does not seem to have been idle, however. Walton tells us that during a period of two years when Donne and his wife were living with Anne's cousin, Sir Francis Woolley, Donne made himself expert in civil and canon law. After Woolley's death, Donne, who was now reconciled with his father-in-law, and receiving an allowance from him, took a house at Mitcham, and lodgings in the Strand, where he seems to have acted as a consultant (possibly a legal expert), and where he also may have helped Thomas Morton (later Dean of Gloucester and Bishop of Durham) in anti-Catholic polemic. Morton even, in 1607, offered him a living: but Donne for the time

1. There is some evidence that Donne may have sat in Parliament for a short period late in 1601, just before his marriage; and that Egerton may have used his influence to get him returned. (See I. A. Shapiro in *T.L.S.*, 10 March 1932, p. 172, 'Was Donne a Member of the 1601 and 1614 Parliaments?').

declined, giving as his reason 'irregularities' in his past life. It is hard to estimate the sincerity of the excuse. Donne continued to be employed as an adviser by important people, and was eventually persuaded by one of his powerful friends, Sir Robert Drury, to move into London, where Drury assigned him and his family a rent-free flat in his own house in Drury Lane. In 1611 Drury insisted that Donne should accompany him on a journey to the continent. Some time before, though it is not certain when, Donne had been presented to James I, who enjoyed his learned conversation and especially his participation in theological discussions. At James's instigation Donne wrote the *Pseudo-Martyr*, an anti-Catholic work, which deals with the question of the advisability of taking oaths of allegiance and supremacy. Donne's friends had attempted to persuade James to give Donne secular employment, and the Earl of Somerset tried to obtain for him one of the Clerkships of the Council: but James was determined to prefer Donne ecclesiastically. He almost begged Donne to take orders (1612), but Donne did not do so till the beginning of 1615.[1] Meanwhile, according to Walton, he studied Divinity, Greek and Hebrew. When he finally took orders, the King made him his Chaplain-in-ordinary, and promised to pay particular attention to his preferment; a promise which was amply fulfilled.

We may now briefly consider Donne's writings during this second period (1598–1614). The verse includes the fifth Satire (against the bribing of judges) (*c.* 1599) and a few of the *Elegies*, notably *The Autumnal*, a very fine Platonic love-poem written to Mrs Herbert, possibly about 1608. Then there are many verse-letters, some in a tone of equality to intimate friends like Roland Woodward or the Brookes, and some in a vein of hyperbolical compliment to socially elevated persons, especially women, like the Countesses of Bedford and Huntingdon. It is more than likely that some of these were intended partly, even if only indirectly, to advance his social position and career in the lean years. Donne also wrote during this period a number of *Epicedes* and *Obsequies*, mainly on socially distinguished people, and in 1611–12, probably as an act of gratitude to his patron, Sir Robert Drury, he penned the two *Anniversaries* on the death of Drury's daughter, Elizabeth.

1. There is evidence that Donne may have sat in Parliament again from 5 April to 7 June 1614, when Parliament was dissolved.

These contained such high-flown tributes that Ben Jonson called them 'blasphemous'. Donne then explained to Jonson that he had been describing the 'idea of a Woman', not an individual. The *Epithalamions* for Princess Elizabeth and for the Earl of Somerset (both 1613) are occasional poems of no great merit, possibly written to order. A good deal earlier in the period (in 1601) Donne had written part of *The Progress of the Soul*, an extraordinary satirical poem tracing the progress of the soul of heresy from its origins in the apple of Eden, through many animal forms, to its final human state in the arch-heretic, Queen Elizabeth. It is probable that the poem sprang from Donne's shock and discontent at the execution of his old commander, Essex, in February 1601. In this poem Donne reaches the most exaggerated height of his 'metaphysical' style, turning all his learning to the most extraordinary purposes, while maintaining a general tone of absurdity in keeping with his satiric purpose. Finally, as already indicated, many of the *Divine Poems* probably belong to the latter part of the period (1607–14). These include *La Corona* (*c.* 1607), almost all the *Holy Sonnets* (?1609), *A Litany* (?1608), and a number of short poems, among which *Goodfriday, 1613. Riding Westward*, is particularly noteworthy, as showing Donne's state of mind at a time quite close to the date of his ordination. These divine poems are no less instinct with passion, imagery, learning, and intellectual subtlety than the secular poems of the same period.

The chief prose works of this second period are the curious *Biathanatos* (written after 1606 and before 1609), the *Pseudo-Martyr* (1610) already mentioned, *Ignatius's Conclave* (written 1610–11; published 1611) and the *Essays in Divinity* (written some time between 1611 and the end of 1614). *Biathanatos* is 'a declaration of that paradox or thesis, that self-homicide is not so naturally sin, that it may never be otherwise'. It is ingeniously argued, and also throws light on Donne's spiritual life. The *Pseudo-Martyr* must be regarded as an occasional work, and *Ignatius's Conclave*, in which Donne attacks the Jesuits in the scurrilous manner characteristic of much of the polemic of the age, though full of clever wit, is not a work of substance. The *Essays in Divinity* are learned, and of great interest as showing Donne's theological difficulties before ordination: but, save in the prayers, they lack both personal urgency and literary value. It is only in the *Biathanatos* and the *Letters* that we find sincere personal interests leavening Donne's wit and learning.

It is perhaps worth noting that with these exceptions it seems to be only in the last period of Donne's life (1615–31), in his period as a priest, that Donne's work in prose attains a quality comparable with that of his best poetry. It is in the *Devotions* and in the *Sermons* that we find once again the ring of strong and true feeling. Here it vivifies the ramifications of his prose, just as it had formerly sustained the complex stanza forms of the *Songs and Sonets*. In the *Sermons*, too, we find elaborated in a masterly way a whole systematic Anglican theology, to which Donne brings all the resources of his learning and sharp intelligence, and the rich and varied imagery which obeys the call of his powerful imagination. His *Sermons* follow a general pattern, rising from exact and forceful exposition to sublime flights of religious prose poetry. Donne's genius had been directed into a new form, and had succeeded in filling it out. The *Sermons*, however, though they are likely to be read more when the great edition now in preparation is complete,[1] will probably never have the universal appeal that the *Songs and Sonets* may eventually achieve. Fine as the *Sermons* are, and overwhelming as was their effect when Donne delivered them, there is in them too much of the outmoded weight of seventeenth-century theology, and they are too long, for them to become general reading for the public of modern times.

III. GROUPINGS WITHIN THE 'SONGS AND SONETS'

There are fifty-five *Songs and Sonets*, if we accept Grierson's canon. They offer a somewhat bewildering variety: but they are susceptible of various sorts of classification.

One way of classifying them which may be found illuminating is according to the predominating attitudes expressed. It is then possible to make a broad division of the poems into (1) those in which the predominating attitude is *negative*, and (2) those in which it is *positive*. By (1) I mean poems in which the poet expresses an overall hostility to love, to women, to some particular woman, or indeed to anybody or anything: and by (2) I mean poems in which the poet

1. The Sermons of John Donne, ed. G. R. Potter and E. M. Simpson, 10 vols., University of California, 1953– (Vol. I, 1953; Vol. VI, 1953; Vol. VII, 1954; Vol. II, 1955; Vol. VIII, 1956; Vol. III, 1957; Vol. IX, 1958).

expresses some buoyant outlook upon love or woman, or in which he courts or praises some woman, or deals sympathetically with the growth of love, or expresses satisfaction with a love which appears settled for some time at least, or fear lest that valued love should cease or the loved person be lost through death, or in which the overall attitude is, in general, one of love, liking, approval, or something similar, towards anyone or anything.[1]

Let us first consider the *Songs and Sonets* in Class (1), the *negative* poems. These can be conveniently sub-classified as follows:

(1) (*a*) Poems in which the hostility is expressed in general terms, not as hostility towards some particular person or relationship. These poems are: the *Song*, 'Go and catch a falling star', *Love's Usury*, *Mummy* or *Love's Alchemy*, *Farewell to Love*, *The Curse*, and perhaps the fragment ⟨*The Rejection*⟩ or ⟨*Self-love*⟩.[2] It is an indication of the marvellous variety of the *Songs and Sonets* that the first four of these poems, all expressing hostility to love, are quite distinct in their main point, in the type of hostility expressed, in the incidental thoughts and feelings, and in the forms used, which vary from the comparative simplicity of the lyric *Song* to the tortuous complexity of the difficult *Farewell to Love*.

(1) (*b*) Poems in which the hostility is directed towards some particular woman or relationship. These poems are: *Woman's Constancy*, *The Triple Fool*, *Twickenham Garden*, *The Message*, *Love's Exchange*, *The Apparition* (the most venomously bitter of all the *Songs and Sonets*), *Love's Deity*, *Love's Diet*, *The Will*, *The Funeral*, *The Blossom*, *A Jet Ring Sent*. The moods expressed in these poems are very various. *The Triple Fool* is the mildest, the hostility being almost dissolved in bland humour. *The Will* is a *tour de force* of wit, and the ingenuity of the conceits diverts attention from the underlying dissatisfaction, which remains, however, as a sort of ground-bass, and makes itself separately heard at the end of each stanza, and in the greater part of the last stanza of all. This poem affords a sharp contrast with *The Apparition*, in which no

1. For other classifications of the *Songs and Sonets* see, for instance, Grierson's edition of Donne's Poetical Works, Oxford, 1912, II. 9–10; and Mr J. B. Leishman's *The Monarch of Wit*, 174–5.

2. The brackets ⟨ ⟩ enclosing these titles indicate that the titles were not given to the poem by Donne, but are the inventions of modern editors, in the absence of any title.

flight of fancy diffuses or relieves the deadly controlled fury: though even here there is some element of poised irony blended with the rage, which makes the onslaught all the more effective. Not so very far in mood and concentration from *The Apparition* we have *Woman's Constancy*, which is, however, distinguished from it by the complete detachment of the last few lines, in which Donne throws off the relationship with a play on two senses of 'lunatic'—(1) inconstant person; (2) madly foolish person—and a scornful shrug:

> Vain lunatic, against these 'scapes I could
> Dispute, and conquer, if I would;
> Which I abstain to do,
> For by tomorrow, I may think so too.

Twickenham Garden, *The Funeral*, and *The Blossom* stand somewhat apart from the other poems in this sub-class. *Twickenham Garden* was almost certainly written to the Countess of Bedford, and seems to express the hostility arising from a rebuff against an attempt by the poet to sexualize a Platonic relationship. *The Funeral* and *The Blossom* may (though the point is the subject of controversy[1]) have been addressed to Mrs Herbert, and seem, in any case, to be of a somewhat similar nature to *Twickenham Garden*.

I have named eighteen poems as poems in Class (1), the class of *negative* poems. This is only about one-third of the total number of *Songs and Sonets*. The majority of the *Songs and Sonets*, then, are to be reckoned as poems expressing some kind of *positive* attitude. It is, however, to be remembered that I have included among 'positive' attitudes a buoyant outlook upon love or women, and one form of buoyant outlook is an attitude of glorious and irresponsible inconstancy. There are also one or two poems which it is hard to classify in either class. I shall say a word or two about these later. Neither qualification to the generalization that the majority of the *Songs and Sonets* express some kind of positive attitude is a very serious one. There are few poems of inconstancy, and only two which seem really neutral.

Let us now consider poems of Class (2), the *positive* poems. These can also be conveniently sub-classified, as follows:

(2) (*a*) Poems expressing an attitude of inconstancy. The poems in this group are: *The Indifferent*, *Community*, *Confined Love*. (The

1. See note 1 on p. xviii.

negative poem, *Woman's Constancy*, however, borders on this group by virtue of its ending.)

(2) (*b*) Courting poems. These are: *Lovers' Infiniteness*, *The Legacy* (which I think belongs here rather than among the poems of (1) (*b*)), *Air and Angels*, *The Dream*, *The Flea*, *The Bait*, *The Broken Heart* (a subtle example of an oblique courting poem), *The Ecstasy* (another subtle example, the whole 'dialogue of one' from l. 29 to the end of the poem being, I believe, an attempt to convince his lady of the advisability of 'going to bodies' by suggesting that she already sees the wisdom of doing so), *The Primrose*, *The Damp*, *The Prohibition*, *The Computation*, (*Sonnet*) *The Token*. There are thus only a round dozen of courting poems among the *Songs and Sonets*, a rather small proportion.

(2) (*c*) Poems expressing satisfaction in a love relationship. In this sub-class I should put: *The Good-morrow*, *The Sun Rising*, *The Canonization*, *The Anniversary*, *Love's Growth*, and *The Undertaking*, which differs from the other poems in that it concerns a Platonic love. One should perhaps also include in this group *The Relic*, which, on the most plausible interpretation, also expresses satisfaction in a Platonic love. One could perhaps include, in addition, on the periphery of this group, *A Lecture upon the Shadow*, in which Donne expresses anxiety that a satisfying love should last. The same care for the future of a precious relationship appears in *The Good-morrow* and *The Anniversary*, as a corollary to the satisfaction expressed, so that there is a definite link between these poems and *A Lecture upon the Shadow*.

(2) (*d*) Poems of parting. There are eight of these: 'Sweetest love, I do not go', *Break of Day*, *A Valediction: of my name, in the window*, *A Valediction: of the book*, *A Valediction: of weeping*, *Witchcraft by a Picture*, *A Valediction: forbidding mourning*, and *The Expiration*. *Break of Day* differs from the other poems of the group in virtue of its being clearly an *aubade*, and of its being put into the mouth of the lady. The other poems of the group vary somewhat in character, and also in value. The best are undoubtedly the *Song*, 'Sweetest love, I do not go', *A Valediction: of weeping* and *A Valediction: forbidding mourning*. Between *A Valediction: of weeping* and the other two poems, there is, however, a marked contrast. *A Valediction: of weeping* is a tempestuous poem; the moods shift sharply, the lines change length, and the last stanza of the poem contradicts the ten-

dency of the first. *A Valediction: forbidding mourning*, on the other hand, stands out by its lofty and compelling restraint, and the even tenor of its movement. The *Song* is more lissom, but the overall mood is similar in its freedom from turbulence. We know that *A Valediction: forbidding mourning* was written by Donne to his wife in 1612, and it is tempting to believe that the finely felt *Song* and the passionate *Valediction: of weeping* sprang from the same relationship.

(2) (*e*) Poems in which a satisfactory love is threatened or attacked by death. These poems are: *A Fever*, *A Nocturnal upon St Lucy's Day* (perhaps the finest of all the *Songs and Sonets*), and *The Dissolution*.

I have now classified fifty-three out of the fifty-five *Songs and Sonets*, and we are left with the two poems, *Negative Love* or *The Nothing*, and *The Paradox*. *Negative Love* is rather a paradoxical analysis of a way of loving than the expression of an attitude: but if any attitude is expressed it is probably better to call it 'neutral' than 'positive' or 'negative'. *The Paradox* is probably best regarded as an 'evaporation of wit', but it could possibly be classified as a poem of Class 2 (*b*), as a poem of oblique courtship like *The Broken Heart*.

I believe that this is one valid way of sorting the *Songs and Sonets* into kinds. There are, as we have seen, borderline cases; but that is to be expected, and need not disturb us.

A classification of this sort, however, though I think it helps us to grasp more easily the variety of the *Songs and Sonets*, leaves much to be said about them: in the following section an attempt will be made to deal with some other leading aspects of the poems.

IV. SOME LEADING FEATURES OF THE 'SONGS AND SONETS'

One of the most striking features of the *Songs and Sonets* is undoubtedly the way in which the most diverse thoughts, images and allusions are pressed into the service of love poetry. References are made to such varied fields as astronomy, law, religion, war and military affairs, medicine, eating and drinking, the human body, time, marriage and divorce, the weather, scholastic philosophy, politics, alchemy, death, fire and heat, astrology, business, learning, and everyday home life. Very often there is an astonishing difference between the field to which reference is made and the context in which the reference appears in the poem. A celebrated instance is Donne's comparison of himself and his wife to a pair of compasses. Another particularly striking instance occurs in *A Fever*, a poem which deals with the illness of some woman to whom the poet seems greatly attached. The Stoics had disputed among themselves as to what sort of fire would consume the world at the end of each cycle of existence; and a similar controversy about the origin and nature of a world-consuming fire had occurred in the theology of the Early Christian era. Donne deliberately makes a preposterous use of that old dispute:

> O wrangling schools, that search what fire
> Shall burn this world, had none the wit
> Unto this knowledge to aspire,
> That this her fever might be it?
>
> (*A Fever*, ll. 13–16)

The turn of wit adds a special strengthening savour to the poignancy of the poem. Even the most far-fetched references generally seem compellingly apt within their context in the poems. The combination of surprise and aptness is certainly one of the chief merits of the imagery and allusion in the *Songs and Sonets*.

It was possibly more especially Donne's references to scholastic philosophy that led Dryden to censure him for affecting metaphysics even 'in his amorous verses, where nature only should reign'. It was probably this censure that brought into currency the application of the term 'metaphysical' to the poetry of Donne and his followers. But the term 'metaphysical' soon acquired a more general sense than Dryden probably intended, and came to connote the employment of learning as the stuff of poetry. Later still, the term, owing to its traditional association with the work of particular poets such as Donne, Crashaw and Cowley, acquired a still broader connotation, namely the body of characteristics common and peculiar to the work of those English poets whom tradition has called 'metaphysical'. Thus the term 'metaphysical imagery', for instance, would now be quite commonly understood to refer to imagery which was *inter alia* both far-fetched and apt, like much of that of such poets as Donne, Crashaw and Cowley.

The effect of the diversity of reference in the *Songs and Sonets* is often increased by the rapidity with which reference to one field succeeds reference to another sometimes very different field. Noteworthy examples occur in the last stanzas of *The Relic* and *The Broken Heart*.

Equally characteristic of the *Songs and Sonets* is the marked absence of mythological and pastoral imagery and allusion. This was early recognized as a general characteristic of Donne's poetry. It was, no doubt, partly to this feature that Carew was referring in the following lines from his admirable Elegy on Donne's death:

> The Muses' garden with pedantic weeds
> O'erspread, was purg'd by thee; the lazy seeds
> Of servile imitation thrown away,
> And fresh invention planted.
>
> (Carew's *Elegy* on Donne's death, ll. 25–8)

This absence of mythological and pastoral allusion entails the absence of conventional remoteness and gallantry from the *Songs and Sonets*. In their place a firm and even a stern realism is often imparted to the poems by the references to war and military affairs, death, law, politics, medicine, fire and heat, business, the human body, and many of the features of home life: while, on the other hand, a certain lofty, *recherché* strain is often provided by the references to Scholastic doctrine, astronomy, religion, and learning: and a less lofty strangeness is injected by the references to alchemy, astrology and superstition.

The *Songs and Sonets* are also remarkable for the strength and range of the feelings they express. There is the incandescent but controlled fury of *The Apparition*; there is the violent allergy to love expressed in *Love's Usury*; there is the uprush of poignant longing in the opening lines of *A Fever*; there is the turbulent sadness of parting in *A Valediction: of weeping*; there is the protective tenderness of the *Song*, 'Sweetest love, I do not go'; there is the firm confidence in mutual love which pervades *A Valediction: forbidding mourning*; there is the desolate grief of *A Nocturnal upon St Lucy's Day*.

Besides the overall variety of the feeling expressed in the *Songs and Sonets* as a whole, there is also often (though not always) considerable variety of feeling within individual poems. One especially interesting type of case is where negative feelings like petulance, bitterness, cynicism, irritation or contempt arise in the course of poems which are predominantly positive. *The Sun Rising* is a happy poem of consummated love: but it is strewn with insults and scornful references. *The Canonization* is a vigorous glorification of love, but it begins with a voluminous outpouring of exasperation and contempt. Even in *Lovers' Infiniteness*, where the wooing is conducted on the whole in a tone of gentle reasonableness, there are overtones of petulance in places, e.g. in the use of such words as 'bargain' (l. 8), 'stocks' (l. 16) and 'outbid' (l. 17), which introduce the bitter suggestion of a love-market. If the matter is looked into it will be found that there is scarcely a single positive poem into which some such feeling as cynicism, bitterness or contempt does not to some degree intrude. This strengthens the poems: for just as when a hard man weeps it is impressive, so it is when a sceptical or cynical man loves.

It should be added that the feeling in the *Songs and Sonets* as a whole gives a strong impression of masculinity. Lovers may die in these poems, but they do not faint, as they do in Keats and Shelley. The language is generally manly and vigorous, and sometimes sudden, or even harsh. The detailed reference to such masculine activities as war and politics also contributes to the total impression of masculine feeling.

On the other hand, contrary to a fairly widespread idea about them, the *Songs and Sonets*, though they often express or imply the view that physical passion is a good thing, yet (in contrast with the *Elegies*) rather seldom express actual feelings of physical lust. This is one of the ways in which the *Songs and Sonets* are distinguishable from much of the work of those other great love poets, Ovid, Propertius and Ronsard.

Another leading feature of the *Songs and Sonets* is their rather peculiar sensory atmosphere. They contain very little colour: though there are, from time to time, remarkably sharp, colourless visual impressions. Even these, however, are exceptional, and the focus of attention is very rarely the visual aspect of experience. The rarity of auditory sensations is even more marked. There is nothing in the whole of the *Songs and Sonets* like Wordsworth's 'casual shout that broke the silent air', or Vigny's

J'aime le son du cor, le soir, au fond des bois.

There is, indeed, scarcely any reference to sounds at all.[1] Again, sense-impressions of smell as distinct from taste do not seem to occur in the *Songs and Sonets*. There are, on the other hand, a few references to sensations of taste, and a fair number to the motor sensations involved in sucking, feeding, drinking, and swallowing. This strain of often rather coarse physicality gives its definite tang to the poems in which it occurs, and sometimes contrasts strangely with the intellectual and spiritual interests which lie beside it. Other motor sensations are frequently referred to, e.g. the sensations involved in running, walking, snatching, winking, leaning. So also are organic sensations, such as the sense of inflammation of the veins which love may cause, or the sensation of 'sorrowing dulness' after sexuality. In point of fact, in the *Songs and Sonets* motor and organic sensations definitely predominate over sensations of sight, sound, smell, taste, and even touch, and that is so even if we include in 'touch' cutaneous sensations of temperature as well as those of pressure. This probably helps to account for a feeling of *inwardness* that one quite frequently senses in the poems, despite all their references to the outside world.

With regard to what psychologists would call the 'feeling-tone' of the poems, painful sense-impressions are quite often stimulated in the course of poems which are predominantly pleasurable. This is a parallel feature to that already noted in the case of feelings.

The use of language in the *Songs and Sonets* has also some special features. The diction (as contrasted with the thought) is generally simple: though Donne often combines the simple words in unexpected ways, forming strange compounds or odd phrases or sentences:

And makes one little room, an *everywhere*.
(*The Good-morrow*, l. 11)

Thou art so *truth*, . . .
(*The Dream*, l. 7)

1. The verse itself, on the other hand, provides interesting sound effects; but that is quite a different matter, which will be considered later.

A *she-sigh* from my mistress' heart, . . .
(*Love's Diet*, l. 10)

And if some lover, such as we,
Have heard this *dialogue of one*, . . .
(*The Ecstasy*, ll. 73–4)

No *tear-floods*, nor *sigh-tempests* move; . . .
(*A Valediction: forbidding mourning*, l. 6)

But since this god produc'd a destiny,
And that *vice-nature*, custom, lets it be; . . .
(*Love's Deity*, ll. 5–6)

Sometimes he puns, though punning does not appear to be frequent. Sometimes he repeats words or types of phrase, throwing them up like a juggler. He is particularly fond of playing with pronouns and demonstrative adjectives:

Coming and staying show'd thee, thee,
But rising makes me doubt, that now
Thou art not thou.
(*The Dream*, ll. 21–3)

To me thou, falsely, thine,
And I to thee mine actions shall disguise.
(*A Lecture upon the Shadow*, ll. 20–1)

This sort of passage gives a combined impression of virtuosity and intimacy.

From time to time, though rather seldom, Donne deviates from the normal simplicity of the diction, by employing learned language: and on such occasions the work takes on a certain sophistication. On the other hand, he more frequently interpolates coarse diction, which imparts to the poetry a rasping force. On other occasions special effects are obtained by the use of words with associations that are homely rather than coarse:

Because such fingers need to *knit*
That subtle *knot*, which makes us man: . . .
(*The Ecstasy*, ll. 63–4)

If he wrung from me a tear, I *brin'd* it so
With scorn or shame, that him it nourish'd not; . . .
(*Love's Diet*, ll. 13–14)

Donne occasionally achieves a peculiar effect of some subtlety by veiling the full meaning of a word or phrase which is really charged with intense implications. One example occurs in the first stanza of *Love's Usury*. Donne is there bargaining with Love, and begging Love not to ensnare him till middle-age, but meanwhile to allow him to give full rope to the caprices of lust:

> Till then, Love, let my body reign, and let
> Me travel, sojourn, snatch, plot, have, forget,
> Resume my last year's relict: think that yet
> We'd never met. (ll. 5–8)

The true import of the intensely contemptuous word 'relict', viz. cast-off mistress, is veiled under its apparent generality. Other instances are the phrase 'think Thou call'st for more' (meaning more sexual play) in ll. 8–9 of *The Apparition*, and the word 'mistake' (meaning mistake and sleep with) in l. 11 of *Love's Usury*: both of which have an uncanny pregnancy. It is also possible that there is a very bold instance of this technique in stanza 2 of *The Relic*: for it is not out of the question that the vague phrase 'a something else thereby' (l. 18) may really mean a bone of Christ's.

The general tone of the language of the *Songs and Sonets* is colloquial. The poems have the flexibility and liveliness of spoken language. The openings are often particularly colloquial in tone. This has the effect of making the poems seem to grow naturally out of definite situations in individual lives. Sentences, on the other hand, are generally somewhat longer than one would expect to find in ordinary speech. Yet Donne manages to keep the vital and passionate phrases he writes, in continuity with one another, so as to form wholes which have both firmness and shape.

Donne is acutely alive to the sound-values of words: and the sound is sometimes almost magically interwoven with the sense. Particularly striking instances of this are to be found in *The Expiration*, *The Apparition*, *Twickenham Garden*, *Mummy* or *Love's Alchemy*, and *A Nocturnal upon St Lucy's Day*.

Everywhere in the poems are to be found instances of rapid and ingenious thinking. The Protean changes of imagery and allusion have already been mentioned. There is also a strong tendency to the violence of paradox, and to the sort of convolution of thought exemplified in the following lines from *Love's Exchange*:

Love, let me never know that this
Is love, or, that love childish is;
Let me not know that others know
That she knows my pains, lest that so
A tender shame make me mine own new woe.
(ll. 17–21)

Typical, too, is the kind of intellectual juggling we find in the clever play on personal identity in stanza 2 of *The Legacy*:

I heard me say: 'Tell her anon,
That my self' (that is you, not I)
'Did kill me'; and when I felt me die,
I bid me send my heart, when I was gone;
But I alas could there find none,
When I had ripp'd me, and search'd where hearts did lie; . . .
(ll. 9–14)

What is remarkable is that such intellectual acrobatics seldom detract from the overall strength of the poems in which they occur. Indeed they often add to it, and sometimes even (as e.g. in *The Primrose*) form a central part of the total effect.

The intellectual agility and ingenuity of the poems are special manifestations of an intellectual strength also shown in other ways, and especially in the relevance and tight concatenation of the thought throughout almost all the poems. Each poem has its specific conception, its focal centre, and there is very rarely any drifting away from the point, however diverse the objects which are referred to, or the images and ideas which occur. This is true both in the simplest sort of case, such as *The Apparition*, where the whole poem of seventeen lines consists of one sentence of concentrated ironic loathing; and in the most complex sort of case, such as that of *A Nocturnal upon St Lucy's Day*, where allusions of considerable diversity and subtlety are strewn thickly through the poem, affording intellectual satisfaction in themselves, but no less certainly contributing to the emotional and intellectual totality of the poem. Where there is apparent irrelevance it is almost certain to serve some deliberate purpose, as in the brilliant effect of the last two lines of *The Curse*. As to the concatenation of the thought within the poems, this is almost everywhere controlled and sure. It has sometimes even been said that the texture of the *Songs and Sonets* is argumentative. This is too sweeping a generalization. The thought arises at the start from the situation out of which the poem itself grows, and it then develops, sometimes indeed by way of argument, but at other times by way of narrative, or analogy, or extended metaphor, or through the play of fancy, or at the prompting of some fresh feeling which has come into play, or in some other way; though almost always so that the connections of the thought are close, whether this is obvious or appears only after scrutiny.

With regard to the attitudes towards love expressed or implied in the poems, their variety has already been indicated. (See Section III, above.) It is, however, worth noticing certain other important features of these attitudes. For one thing, there runs through the *Songs and Sonets*, taken as a whole, the belief that physical passion is a good thing. Sometimes, especially in the apparently earlier poems, it is seen as good in itself, even, at times, as preferable to the perils of love. Sometimes it is seen as a necessary and valuable element in a full and satisfying mutual attachment. For another thing, love is generally considered in these poems either as a danger or as a wonder. It is not thought of coolly as something that can be handled or trifled with, and seldom thought of simply as one of the pleasures of life. We are most often in the realm of *amour passion*, comparatively rarely in the realm of *amour physique*, and never in that of *amour goût*, to make use of Stendhal's illuminating distinctions.[1] Passionate feeling is paramount; even *passionate* sensuality is secondary; mere elegant gallantry (so frequent in Restoration love-lyrics) is completely absent.

Again, there are one or two special thoughts about love, which recur in a number of the poems. One is that love is a mystery in which Donne and his lady are adepts. The most extensive expression of this thought occurs in *The Ecstasy*. Clearly linked with it is Donne's practice of crediting his beloved with religious significance, as in *The Relic*, *A Nocturnal upon St Lucy's Day* and *Air and Angels*. In *The Dream* he even goes so far as to maintain that his lady has some of the divine attributes. This practice seems to associate some of the poems with the tradition of the *amour courtois*. Another typical thought is that two lovers are self-sufficient. Donne sometimes hyperbolically extends this idea, and asserts that together they are the whole world. In this way some of the poems become

1. See Stendhal, *De l'Amour*, where the distinctions are fully discussed.

more than love poems: they become glorifications of love. On the other hand, Donne tends to be temperate in his forecast of the future of a love already in existence. We do not find him saying that it will last for ever, or even for a long time. He does express hope that a love will continue, but when he expresses a faith that it will, the faith is only a hypothetical one. 'If you and I love equally, and take care, our love will continue.' This is what Donne says in several places. Statements of this sort are indeed almost tautologous: but these near-tautologies seem much more satisfyingly near the truth than rash categorical faith in eternal constancy. Another, rather subtle, way in which Donne's thought about love distinguishes itself from more commonplace views, is in his uncertainty as to how far lovers are really united by their love (see *A Valediction: forbidding mourning*, *The Ecstasy* (ll. 41–56) and *The Good-morrow* (ll. 20–1)). This uncertainty should, I believe, be regarded as the sign of an honest attempt not to exaggerate about the relationship of love, while at the same time recognizing its unifying force.

Finally, something must be said as to the forms and metres of the poems. The forms are almost all stanzaic. They are exceedingly various, and many of them are very complex. There is only one stanza form that Donne uses more than once: the simple octosyllabic quatrain with alternate rhymes, which he uses in three poems. It seems that over forty of the stanza forms were probably invented by him. The vast majority of the poems are in stanzas of from six to eleven lines. Eight- and nine-line stanzas occur most frequently. Occasionally two or three poems have the same rhyme scheme; but where that is so, they differ in line-length. It is as if Donne proudly scorned to repeat the same stanza form.

Donne is fond of reiterated rhymes. Eighteen of the poems, for instance, end in triplets or quadruplets. This gives an effect of insistence. Again, over twenty of the poems begin with a couplet; and the opening rhyme-scheme *aabb* is very common. The use of reiterated rhymes, whether in the openings or endings or in the body of the poems, acts as a counterforce to the strong tendency in many of the poems for the metric form to be distorted by the speech-rhythms which cut across it. The verse might so easily break into utter disorder. Reiterated rhymes help to prevent this. The triplets in ll. 5–7 of each stanza of *A Nocturnal upon St Lucy's Day* afford an instance of their steadying effect.

Some of the stanza forms are very attractive in themselves. Much play is made with variations of line length. Stanzas of more than six lines seem to give Donne the scope he so often needs to develop the complex interplay of thought and feeling which is so typical of him. With exceptions, the poems in shorter stanzas tend to be thin or slight.

In some cases the stanza forms seem especially appropriate to their respective poems. This is so, for instance, with the *Song*, 'Go and catch a falling star', where the piquant slightness of the short lines prepares by contrast the elongated sting in the tail of each stanza. A similar effect is achieved in *The Blossom*, where the short sixth line of each stanza sets off the epigrammatic couplet which follows. Again, the sharp changes of line length in *A Valediction: of weeping* accord magnificently with the turbulent passion underlying the poem: while the steady fixity of the lines of *A Valediction: forbidding mourning* is at one with the firm and substantial love in which the poem shows such settled confidence. The stanza forms do not always seem so peculiarly appropriate as in these cases: but they frequently delight by their intricacy; and the fact that the rich texture of passion, thought and imagery, and the odd quirks and ironies, could be made to take on shapes of such fairly strict complexity, is often a subject for wonder.

The overall forms of the poems are sometimes very clearly patterned, as in the ternary forms of *The Message*, the *Song*, 'Go and catch a falling star', *Lovers' Infiniteness* and *The Prohibition*. At other times there is no apparent relation between the number of stanzas and the substance of the poem. In most cases, however, the poems give one a definite impression of firm shape. Sometimes, as in the device of the 'dialogue of one' in *The Ecstasy*, and the wonderful thematic modification of the opening line of *A Nocturnal* at the close of the poem, we come across especially satisfying examples of formal beauty.

The metres are normally iambic: but the actual rhythms which play over the basic metrical structure are very various. Drummond tells us that Ben Jonson said that 'for not keeping of accent' Donne 'deserved hanging'. In saying this, however, Jonson only revealed one of his own limitations. Remarkable literary man though Jonson was, the validity of Donne's use of true speaking language springing straight from passion and vigorous and subtle thinking, and not to be strait-laced by the demands of external metres, was beyond him. In point of fact, Donne's verse is generally more regular than Jonson's statement would suggest: provided we construe regularity more liberally than Jonson did. Let us consider, for instance, the fine bitter opening of *Twickenham Garden*. Syllabically, the first two lines are quite regular. The first has ten syllables: the second eight. Pedally, on the other hand, they are admittedly far from being examples of the basic lines, the iambic pentameter and the iambic tetrameter.

Blásted with síghs, | and surr | oúnded with téars,

is best scanned as shown, i.e. as two choriambic feet separated by a pyrrhic.[1]

Híther I cóme | to séek | the spríng.

is best scanned as a choriambus followed by two iambic feet. Only cramping pedantry, however, could find these lines anything but excellent. If the whole poem had been written in lines of the same types as these (which would have been one way of 'regularizing' them!), then it would have been hopelessly monotonous; and the pedal character of these particular lines, which is in complete keeping with their meaning and feeling, would have lost its point. In actual fact, the lines, though pedally irregular, are made to seem regular enough: partly because, syllabically, they *are* regular; partly because the first line has a regularity of its own, since it is perfectly symmetrical, and the second line repeats the choriambic rhythm which has been set up; and partly because the lines merge at once into the general iambic pattern, since the last two feet of the second line are both iambic, and the third line is a regular iambic line. What is more, they satisfy us, in any case, by their force and naturalness, so that we are not inclined to think cantankerously about rules. This is a particularly striking example of Donne's regular irregularity; but it would be possible to cite countless instances from the poems. The *Songs and Sonets* are little short of miraculous in

1. This was apparently in part pointed out by a contemporary of Donne's, Giles Oldisworth, in his notes on Donne. (See John Sampson, 'Contemporary Light upon John Donne' (Essays and Studies of the English Association, vii. 87)).

their blend of the freedom and vitality of the spoken language with the reasonable exigencies of metrical form.

V. THE 'SONGS AND SONETS' AND THE TRADITION OF THE ENGLISH LOVE-LYRIC

The *Songs and Sonets* offer sharp contrasts with the love-lyrics of Donne's predecessors in the sixteenth century.

Wyatt's love poems indeed also abound in colloquial phraseology, and bear the imprint of a strongly individual personality. But the personality is a very different one from Donne's. In most of Wyatt's love poems the poet seems, like Pandarus, to 'hop alway behind' in the game of love. He is almost always complaining. Donne seldom complains: and he never *merely* complains, as Wyatt does. Donne also expresses countless moods which never arise in Wyatt. Wyatt's poems are also far simpler than Donne's both formally and in substance. There is nothing in them of Donne's vast range of reference to life and speculation; and, although many of them have great charm and even power, their structure is rudimentary compared with the poems of Donne.

Surrey was undoubtedly a more accomplished technician than Wyatt, but, in spite of this, and of Surrey's greater range of allusion, his poems are, if anything, still more different from Donne's. Surrey's world is a fresh green world, the world of the wild forest, 'the clothed holt with green', the world of Windsor and the 'palme-play'. Moreover, his learning, when it appears, consists of a few classical allusions. Above all, the spirit of his love poems is almost uniformly that of a patient sufferer from absence or disdain, willing to endure the utmost penalty:

> Sweet is his death that takes his end by love.

Again, Surrey sometimes praises the beauty of his mistress, and laments beauty's passing. The *Songs and Sonets* only praise beauty in one or two instances, and that indirectly, and they never lament its passing. In point of form, moreover, the work of Surrey, though technically proficient, shows none of Donne's virtuosity.

The love poems of both Wyatt and Surrey are, besides, also largely courting poems, and, as we noted, there are comparatively few such poems among the *Songs and Sonets*.

Sidney's love poems are mostly 'sonnets' in the strict sense, which none of the *Songs and Sonets* are. Yet some of the sonnets of the *Astrophel and Stella* sequence come nearer to Donne's love-lyrics than any other poetry of the time, with the possible exception of the sonnets of Shakespeare. There is a briskness in much of Sidney's work, which resembles that of some of the *Songs and Sonets*. There is also an intensity of passion comparable with that expressed by Donne. There is ingenuity in the imagery, and there is even a strong *goût du paradoxe*. There is plentiful use of the living, spoken language. There are no doubt other resemblances, too: but, when all is said, sharp contrasts remain. In Sidney, for instance, there is no expression of a happy, consummated love, at any level. Again, the imagery and allusion do not form so thick a mixture as in Donne, and they are drawn from a far narrower field of reference. On the other hand, more reference to classical literature and mythology is made in Sidney's poems than in the *Songs and Sonets*. Again, Sidney's work contains more visual impressions. We know that Stella's eyes were black; whereas we do not know the colour of the eyes of any of Donne's women, even of his wife's. Sidney's sensory reference, as a whole, however, has less body than that of Donne, and Donne's streak of coarseness is entirely absent. As to ingenuity, though there is plenty in Sidney's work, it does not reach the pitch of Donne's highest turns. Finally, though Sidney was a poet with an excellent ear, his range of music is more confined than Donne's. There is nowhere to be found the powerful resonance of the harmonies of such poems as *The Anniversary* or *A Nocturnal upon St Lucy's Day*. Yet despite the great differences between Sidney's work and Donne's it is hard to believe that there is no significance in the fact that the *Astrophel and Stella* sonnets were printed in 1591, when Donne was just starting his poetical career.

On the other hand, to the Petrarchizing and pastoralizing song and madrigal writers, Donne's early work seems like a vigorous reaction. These conventional poetizings may well have sickened Donne; and this may even account for some of the deliberate coarseness of the *Songs and Sonets* of the earlier period, as well as for some of their harsh realism, and freely vented bitterness and fury. In a few cases we actually find Donne affecting to conform to convention, and then implicitly rejecting it in the course of the same poem. Examples with varying degrees of violence are *The Apparition*, *The*

Message and *The Bait*, in all of which he starts in apparently conventional style, only to play the 'back-trick' on his readers in the course of a few lines.

In 1595 appeared the *Amoretti* and *Epithalamion* of Spenser. Donne had by now commenced poet, though in a very different vein. The splendid *Epithalamion* is, in any case, a marriage hymn, and not fairly comparable with Donne's lyrics. The *Amoretti*, on the other hand, are comparable, though they are sonnets in the strict sense. They differ markedly from the *Songs and Sonets*. They form a strict series. They express and recount a courtship, and a very simple direct type of courtship it is, though it is almost insufferably long. All this contrasts with the work of Donne. Moreover, the courtship proceeds so slowly that there is a fair deal of monotonous repetition of moods. Again, in general, the sonnets are not so intellectually alert as those of Sidney. They have a sensuous, fresh and somewhat naive charm; though even this is marred from time to time by a rather nauseating humility before mere rank. The language used tends towards archaism and formality. These are further differences from Donne. On the other hand, there are occasional instances of imagery similar to that found in the *Songs and Sonets*. For example, in Spenser's Sonnet xv his comparison of his betrothed to 'both the Indias' parallels Donne's reference in ll. 16–18 of *The Sun Rising*. It may be that such references were snapped up by Donne, and turned to his own use: but they are, in any case, few and far between. In general, Spenser's images, unlike Donne's, are inclined to be obvious: not much brain power or experience of life could have been required to bring them into existence. Again, Spenser's persistent reference to the Platonic idea of virtue clad in the form of his betrothed, is briefly parallelled in Donne (e.g. in *The Undertaking*); but it is not for him a dominant theme. Finally, Spenser's limpid movement is utterly diverse from the rapid changes and counterchanges of the verse of Donne; while the tendency to symmetry in Spenser's sonnets is quite alien to the workings of Donne's swift and dynamic feeling and thought.

If, as seems most likely, Meres's reference in 1598 to Shakespeare's 'sugred Sonnets among his private friends' refers to some of the poems we now know as Shakespeare's *Sonnets*, then it is quite possible that Donne may have seen some of them in the late 1590s. There are some images and allusions in Shakespeare's *Sonnets* which resemble images and allusions in the *Songs and Sonets*, e.g. some legal references, and references to mercantile life, to alchemy, to medicine, to food and to the life of the home. There is greater width of reference than in the work of the other lyrists. There is also greater intellectual strength than ever before in the history of the English love-lyric. The feeling, too, is generally intense, and there is in places a harshness of tone, and a physicality and even coarseness of reference, which bring the work at times very close to Donne. Here also we find a taste for paradox at least as strong as Sidney's. The work is also very close to spoken language in vocabulary and structure, and there is a force in it that is certainly nearer to the *Songs and Sonets* than anything in the other poets mentioned. Yet all these similarities are outweighed by the differences. The bulk of Shakespeare's *Sonnets* deal with a relationship with a man. Many of them are concerned simply with expressing Shakespeare's love and regard, or with encouraging his friend to produce children, or with proclaiming the immortality of the *Sonnets* themselves. The sonnets addressed to the 'dark lady' resemble some of the earlier *Songs and Sonets*, especially the negative poems: but the range of attitudes expressed is far narrower than in Donne's lyrics taken as a whole. Again, the *Sonnets* generally possess a smooth texture, which covers the shifts of feeling. There is nothing to correspond to Donne's more complex rhythmic effects. Nor is there, of course, anything to correspond to his wealth of stanza forms. Furthermore, though the range of Shakespeare's references overlaps that of Donne's, the *Sonnets* also direct attention to nature, to mythology, and to a number of elements in the stock-in-trade of Elizabethan poetry which appear to be shunned in the *Songs and Sonets*; while, on the other hand, we do not find in the *Sonnets* the religious or philosophical references characteristic of those *Songs and Sonets* probably assignable to the second period. The comparison of references, moreover, makes it clear who was the more learned poet. Again, though there are resemblances in the sensations referred to (e.g. the many references to eating), the sensory atmosphere of the *Sonnets* contains more visual and auditory elements. Finally, there is, on the whole, a definitely thicker mixture of imagery and allusion in the *Songs and Sonets*, and a more rapid shift from reference to reference, again especially in the apparently later poems. It is only in Shakespeare's *plays* of the Jacobean period that his shift of reference attains such rapidity. There are certainly more distinctions to be drawn: but these are enough to indicate a wide disparity.

Donne's impact on love-poetry was considerable; though it is to be remembered that the best of the other 'metaphysical' poets, Herbert, Crashaw, Vaughan and Marvell, were not primarily love poets. But none of the poets influenced by Donne rivalled the master. Marvell's few love poems, and especially the famous poem *To his Coy Mistress*, are deeply indebted to Donne. Yet they are different enough. The forms Marvell uses are perhaps significant. He writes in short lines, and the verses have a terseness which is, at times, almost telegraphic. There seems to be strong feeling behind some of the work: but it has not the mercurial character or the variety of rhythm of the *Songs and Sonets*. Yet there is no other love poetry influenced by Donne which reaches the level of *To his Coy Mistress*. The love-lyrics of Carew and Lord Herbert of Cherbury and Cowley are probably the next best. Carew was, however, also influenced by the song-writers and by Ben Jonson, and, although there are lines when he suddenly touches unexpected depths, his love-lyrics have too often the appearance of synthetic art. On the other hand, there is a liveliness of apprehension in Carew, and a fanciful ingenuity, which are engaging. But Carew's poems are cheerful, even when they purport to be sad, and, though that feature itself has attractions, it is one measure of the poems' limitations. Carew is most successful when he is rendering the phases of love which are neither passionate nor tragic, where his bright intelligence can play fancifully and gracefully. Lord Herbert seems to write more sincerely: but, on the other hand, his work has not the deftness of Carew's. Neither's work has the depth and variety of true feeling, or the widely ranging, subtle play of intellect embodied in the work of Donne. Cowley's poems have more intellectual brilliance than either Carew's or Lord Herbert's: and, in point of ingenuity of imagery, Cowley's *Hope* and *The Spring* are as fine as any poem by the other two poets. The attitudes expressed by Cowley, however, tend to monotony, and seem often inappropriately unpassionate. His technical excellence and fine turns of thought seem to have nearly monopolized his attention.

The really genuine inspiration in the seventeenth-century love-lyric after the work of Donne does not seem to have come to his imitators, except in the case of one or two poems. It is rather to be found in the hit-and-miss songs of Suckling, and in the miniature creations of Herrick: though both veins are severely limited. After the Restoration, the love-lyric becomes largely a poem of gallantry or seduction (generally a *song*), and the fusion of religion and passionate personal attachment found in the *Songs and Sonets* of Donne's second period, has become unthinkable. As to the eighteenth century, its great love-lyrist was a Scot. It is not till the Romantic period that the *English* love-lyric again comes into its own.

VI. NOTES ON THE TEXT AND CANON

(i) *The Manuscripts*

Very few of the *Songs and Sonets* were printed in Donne's lifetime. On the other hand, it is possible that Eleazar Edgar may have intended to include some of them in his projected *Amours by J. D., with Certen Oyr.* (i.e. other) *sonnettes by W.S.* (? Shakespeare), for which he obtained a licence in 1600. The term 'Amours,' however, may have denoted the *Elegies*; and, in any case, the volume does not seem to have appeared. What is, on the other hand, not merely possible, but even certain, is that some of the *Songs and Sonets* came very near to being printed fourteen years later, just before the time of Donne's ordination. In a letter to his friend Sir Henry Goodyer dated 20 December 1614, Donne tells his friend in a hushed whisper ('so softly that I am loath to hear myself') that he is 'brought to a necessity of printing' his poems, and 'addressing them to the Lord Chamberlain'. It was a question of printing a few copies at his own expense. Donne makes it clear that he was casting around among his friends for copies of his poems, which had been circulated in manuscript, and he asks Goodyer for the loan of an 'old book', in which some of them had obviously been written. Donne wanted the book urgently, for the poems were to be printed 'as a valediction to the world', before he took orders. The inner story of the project remains obscure. It may well be, as Miss Helen Gardner has suggested,[1] that Donne was under considerable pressure from the Lord Chamberlain to publish the poems with a dedication to him. The

1. In her interesting Textual Introduction to her edition of the Divine Poems, Oxford, 1952.

project, however, came to nothing, though why it did so is uncertain.

Donne's poems continued to circulate in manuscript, and, with his growing fame as a cleric, manuscript *collections* of his poems increased rapidly in number. Most of those now available belong to the period 1620–33. This is what we should expect. Donne was made Dean of St Paul's in 1621; and the first edition of his poems appeared in 1633, about two years after his death. Since Donne never again seems to have prepared his poems for the press, and since we have not yet discovered the manuscript, if any, which Donne prepared for publication in 1614, these manuscript collections are of considerable importance for the establishment of an approximation to a true text.

Professor Grierson, in the elaborate textual introduction to his great edition,[1] divided those manuscript collections of Donne's poems which he knew, into three main classes: (1) manuscript collections of Donne's poems; (2) manuscripts containing one or more of Donne's poems without additional matter;[2] and (3) manuscripts containing poems by various authors, including Donne.

As Professor Grierson said,[3] the manuscripts of Class (3) have no authority at all for the textual critic. Moreover, none of the extant manuscripts of Class (2) contains any of the *Songs and Sonets*.

Thus the only manuscripts of importance for us are the manuscript collections of Donne's poems.

These collections Grierson classified into three groups.

Group I contained three manuscripts, closely related to one another:

1. The Dowden MS, now in the library of Mr Wilfred Merton (known as *D*);
2. British Museum, Harleian MS 4955 (known as *H49*);
3. The Leconfield MS, now in the library of Sir Geoffrey Keynes (known as *Lec*).

Since 1912, the date of Grierson's edition, two other manuscripts clearly belonging to this group have turned up:

1. *The Poems of John Donne*, ed. Grierson, Oxford, 1912, II. lvi–cliii.

2. For clarity's sake I should explain that what I am calling Class (1) Grierson calls Class (2), and vice versa. It seemed to me better to put the most important class first in the list.

3. Op. cit., II. cvii.

4. Cambridge University Library, Add. MS 5778 (known as *C57*);
5. St Paul's Cathedral Library, MS 49. B.43 (known as *SP*).

Group II contained four manuscripts, also closely related to one another:

1. British Museum, Add. MS 18647 (known as *A18*);
2. The Norton MS, Harvard College Library, MS Nor. 4503 (known as *N*);
3. Trinity College, Cambridge, MS R.3.12 (known as *TCC*);
4. Trinity College, Dublin, MS G.2.21 (known as *TCD*).

With these four manuscripts Grierson thought that a fifth, which he actually classified in Group III, was closely associated 'at least in parts', viz. British Museum, Landsowne MS 740 (known as *L74*). No fresh manuscript belonging to this group has since come to light.

Group III contained ten manuscripts,[1] of which the most important is the manuscript known as *O'F*.[2] This is the largest manuscript collection of Donne's poems. It is dated 12 October 1632, and it seems likely that it was prepared with a view to publication. Whoever intended to use it was, however, forestalled by the editor of the 1633 edition.

Some more manuscripts assignable to this group have come to light since 1912, namely:

(*a*) The Dobell MS, Harvard College Library, MS Nor. 4506 (known as *Dob*);
(*b*) The King MS, Raphael King, Catalogue 51, Item 73 (known as *K*);
(*c*) The Luttrell MS, now in the library of Sir Geoffrey Keynes (known as *Lut*).

Group III manuscripts do not hang together so closely as the manuscripts of Groups I and II; and it seems likely that they are generally more remote from the text of the poems as ultimately written by Donne.

Miss Helen Gardner has presented a strong case for the view that the manuscripts of Group I all derive from a copy of the

1. Including *L74*.
2. It is so called because it was at one time owned by Rev. T. R. O'Flaherty of Capel, near Dorking, an assiduous and learned nineteenth-century student of Donne.

collection Donne was preparing for publication at the end of 1614.[1]

With regard to the manuscripts of Group II, her view is that these derive from a copy taken from Donne's own papers some time after 1625. Grierson pointed out that a few of the variations of Group II readings from Group I readings look like revisions by Donne himself. Miss Helen Gardner argues that Donne is unlikely to have revised his early poems, particularly his love poems, after taking orders, and suggests that these differences between Group I and Group II readings may perhaps be explained by the hypothesis that when the root manuscript of Group I was copied in 1614 from Donne's collection, he had not completed his revisions for publication.[2] This may well be true; but it does, of course, depend upon the premise (admittedly probable) that Donne is unlikely to have revised his early poems after taking orders.

Like the manuscripts of the other two groups, those of Group III vary in date. One or two of them may even belong to a period before 1620, but most of them were written after that date, and some as late as 1632.

Miss Gardner agrees with Grierson in thinking that Group III manuscripts sometimes preserve earlier versions of poems found in a revised form in manuscripts of Groups I and II. In the case of the *Songs and Sonets*, there are, however, I believe, only a few instances where this could be so. On the other hand, there are cases where one or more Group III manuscripts agree with manuscripts of Group I as against manuscripts of Group II. In such cases, particularly where there are external reasons for thinking that one or more of the Group III manuscripts concerned represent a version of the poem earlier than mid-1614, the Group III manuscripts may afford some support to the theory that the version of Group II is a revision of the version of Group I. Group III manuscripts, however, sometimes agree with Group II against Group I; and the individual manuscripts of Group III often differ, some agreeing with Group I and some with Group II, and there are further complications. The relationships of Group III manuscripts to the manuscripts of Groups I and II seem to be very complex and hard to determine.

1. Op. cit., lxii–lxv. 2. Op. cit., lxvii–lxviii.

(ii) *The early editions*

The first printed edition of Donne's poems came out in 1633, two years after the poet's death.

Professor Grierson has demonstrated the superiority of the text of this edition to that of all the other seventeenth-century editions, and to that of any extant manuscript or single group of manuscripts.[1] Its text of the *Songs and Sonets* was probably printed from a Group I manuscript closely related to *C57*; but there is evidence that the manuscript concerned had been corrected in places to readings identical with those of Group II manuscripts: and it is also probable that the titles, often absent in Group I manuscripts, were inserted in the manuscript from which the 1633 edition was printed. This manuscript was certainly not Donne's own manuscript which he was preparing for publication in 1614: but it may well have been a copy of this belonging to Goodyer, or even Goodyer's 'old book' brought up to date. Next to Donne's own manuscript (if that existed at his death) this manuscript might, in that case, possibly have been the most authoritative single source that the 1633 editor could have tapped for a text representing what Donne ultimately wrote.

On the other hand, as Grierson himself indicated, the 1633 edition is not to be regarded as sacrosanct. Its text of the *Songs and Sonets*, though clearly printed from an excellent manuscript, was quite probably printed from that manuscript alone: and, what is more, errors can always creep in between manuscript and printed text. There are a few cases in which the 1633 editor has patently gone astray, probably rather from using faulty judgment than from technical inaccuracy. There are also cases in which it is possible that Donne's last corrections had not been incorporated in the manuscript from which the 1633 edition was printed. In addition, there is a question which is not raised by either Professor Grierson or Miss Gardner; but which is, I would submit, a substantial question, namely: Would the final version as written by Donne necessarily be in all cases 'the authentic text'?[2]

I believe that the best policy that could be followed in the absence of Donne's own manuscript or a manuscript fully corrected in Donne's own hand, was to take the 1633 edition as the basis of the

1. *The Poems of John Donne*, ed. Grierson, Oxford, 1912, II. cxiv–cxxi.
2. See my short note on this point in Appendix I.

text, as Grierson did; and to correct from the manuscripts where there was strong reason for doing so. Where my own text differs from that of Grierson (apart from the modernized spelling and punctuation), the differences are almost entirely due to an evident difference of opinion, in particular instances, as to whether there is strong reason for correcting the 1633 edition from the manuscripts or not. In such cases I have indicated my departures from Grierson in the Notes, and tried to justify my readings.

The second edition appeared in 1635. Here the *Songs and Sonets* are grouped together for the first time. The edition includes two of the *Songs and Sonets* not included in the 1633 edition; but it also includes among the *Songs and Sonets* two poems almost certainly not by Donne. The 1635 text of the *Songs and Sonets* is, on the whole, not so good as that of the 1633 edition; but that does not mean that it is always inferior. 1635 readings are sometimes as likely to be right as those of 1633; and sometimes they seem superior, taking all relevant factors into consideration. The edition was probably influenced by one or more Group III manuscripts, almost certainly including *O'F*: sometimes definitely for the worse, but not always.

Other editions were issued in 1639, 1649, 1650, 1654 and 1669. Textually none of those editions, except that of 1669, shows any distinct independence of the earlier editions, as far as the *Songs and Sonets* are concerned. The 1669 edition occasionally adopts readings which Grierson himself accepts, and on other occasions provides readings which seem to have at least a fair chance of being the best. In general, however, it is to be regarded as definitely inferior textually to the 1633 edition, to whose readings it does, nevertheless, often revert.

The 1669 edition is, as Grierson indicated, the last edition before the modern editions which shows signs of recourse to manuscripts.

(iii) *The modern editions*

The chief modern editions including the *Songs and Sonets* are those of Grosart (1872–3), Norton (1895), Chambers (1896), Grierson (1912), Mr John Hayward (1929), and Mr R. E. Bennett (1942). Of these the most important, undoubtedly, is Grierson's edition. Grosart's text is very unreliable. He did not use either editions or manuscripts systematically. Norton's edition is vastly superior, both in text and in notes. Norton followed the 1633 edition very closely, but unfortunately he freely altered the punctuation without recording the changes even where sense was affected. Chambers used all the seventeenth-century editions and a few manuscripts. He modernized the spelling and punctuation, and produced some good notes: but changes of punctuation from the old editions are most frequently not recorded, often even when the alteration drastically modifies the meaning: and textually the edition was superseded by Grierson's, which was based on a thorough and systematic collation of the early editions and many manuscripts. Furthermore, though Chambers wrote good notes, he did not write enough of them; and many cruces were left unexplained. Grierson's edition established a text in old spelling and old punctuation, which is unlikely to require radical modification, though it may be open to question on a number of points of detail. Grierson also wrote many illuminating notes: but these were not his primary preoccupation, and they still leave a fair number of dark places. Mr John Hayward's text of the poems, whose preparation involved re-collation of the old editions and many manuscripts, introduces occasional improvements on Grierson's text. Mr Hayward also provides a few explanatory notes. Mr Roger E. Bennett has recently produced a new edition of the Complete Poems in the United States. It is in modern spelling and punctuation, and Mr Bennett has thereby attempted to fulfil a real need. His edition has many merits; but unfortunately he seems often not to have taken sufficient factors into consideration in determining his readings. Moreover, his edition does not contain explanatory notes. Thus there is, as yet, no wholly satisfactory edition of Donne's poems in modern spelling and punctuation, and with explanatory notes.

The present edition is, as far as I know, the first separate edition of the *Songs and Sonets* with explanatory notes. It is in modern spelling, and the punctuation has been modernized, or rather, more strictly speaking, *modified* with the intention of bringing out the full meaning of the poems to a modern reader.[1] Purists who may be horrified at the modification of the punctuation of the 1633 edition (though they seldom seem perturbed by the modification, in

1. Where my punctuation differs from that of Grierson's edition in such a way as to affect the sense, I have indicated the deviation in the Notes.

modern editions of Shakespeare, of the punctuation of the First Folio), may feel pacified by the distinct possibility that the punctuation of the 1633 edition was in fair measure the work of the editor or printer of the edition, and not always the nicely calculated pointing of the poet himself.

NOTE ON THE USE OF THE SLUR

In the early editions and in the manuscripts an apostrophe is often inserted between two words, where there is no question of its standing for a missing letter. In many cases this device is clearly intended to indicate that the two words should be pronounced with scarcely any interval between them. It seems possible that this was Donne's own intention. There is no modern typographical equivalent for the device: and the elision of a letter together with the use of an apostrophe would not generally meet the case. Therefore, in those instances where a modern reader might well fail to obey what may have been Donne's wishes, I have inserted a slur (instead of the old apostrophe), to indicate that there should be virtual continuity in pronunciation.

The
Songs and Sonets
of John Donne

THE GOOD-MORROW

I wonder, by my troth, what thou and I
Did, till we lov'd ? were we not wean'd till then ?
But suck'd on country pleasures, childishly ?
Or snorted we in the Seven Sleepers' den ?
'Twas so; but this, all pleasures fancies be:
If ever any beauty I did see,
Which I desir'd, and got, 'twas but a dream of thee.

And now good-morrow to our waking souls,
Which watch not one another out of fear;
For love, all love of other sights controls,
And makes one little room, an everywhere.
Let sea-discoverers to new worlds have gone,
Let maps to others, worlds on worlds have shown,
Let us possess one world, each hath one, and is one.

My face in thine eye, thine in mine appears,
And true plain hearts do in the faces rest;
Where can we find two better hemispheres,
Without sharp North, without declining West ?
Whatever dies, was not mix'd equally;
If our two loves be one, or, thou and I
Love just alike in all, none of these loves can die.

THE GOOD-MORROW

3 *country*] 'rustic', and therefore, probably, unrefined as compared with the pleasures of the Court or City. The sense here then seems to be: 'Weren't we satisfied in a childish way with pleasures which, when compared with our love, were like those of country people as compared with those of people in the City or at Court?'

4 *snorted*] i.e. snored.
Seven Sleepers' den] The Seven Sleepers were the heroes of a celebrated legend translated from the Syriac by Gregory of Tours, and included in his *De Gloria Martyrum*. The story tells that in A.D. 250 or 251 during the persecution of the Christians by the Emperor Decius, seven Christian youths from Ephesus took refuge in a cave in a nearby mountain. Their pursuers walled up the entrance of the cave, with the intention of starving them to death; but the young men fell into a miraculous sleep, from which they did not wake until some time during the reign of Theodosius II (possibly A.D. 439 or A.D. 446). When they woke, they thought they had only been asleep for a single night, and one of them, who went to the city for food, was amazed to find, on the churches and other buildings, the cross, which, when he had fallen asleep, had been an object of execration.

5 *but*] except.

10] 'For love inhibits all desire to see other people or things.'

13 *worlds*] Either 'continents', or 'worlds' in a sense which would include celestial bodies.

13] 'Let maps have revealed worlds on worlds to other people.'
others] Professor Grierson adopts the reading of the printed editions 1633–54, viz. 'other'. The most reliable MSS, however, read 'others'. The meaning of the two readings is precisely the same; 'other' was a form of plural: but in a modern recension it would, I think, be pointlessly awkward to retain the obsolete form.

14] The meaning of this line is not so clear as it might at first seem. Is there one world, or are there two? The first half of the line suggests that there is *one* world, the world of their mutual love: but the second half of the line suggests that each of the lovers is a world, and the implication would seem to be that there are *two* worlds. Looking into the line closely, therefore, may tend to spoil it for us, but it seems to me that we must look into it: it is a compliment which 'metaphysical' poetry demands. In reading the line we are not much disturbed, because we are caught up by the wonderful tone of conviction: but can we eliminate *all* disturbance? One possible solution seems to me to be that this line is simply an elliptical expression of an uncertainty which Donne expresses elsewhere, as to whether the souls (or the loves) of two lovers are one or two (cf. ll. 20–1 of this very poem, and ll. 21–6 of *A Valediction: forbidding mourning*). There may, however, really be no basic uncertainty here: and in that case another solution of the apparent contradiction in the line would be required. There is perhaps the possibility that the worlds in the second half of the line are *hemispheres*, Donne thereby exploiting still further the ambiguities of 'world' and leading up to l. 17. Finally, however, it must be mentioned that many MSS read 'our world', so that it is *possible* that the whole difficulty arises from the (very simple) misreading of 'one' for 'our' by a copyist.

18] 'Without the North, with its bitter cold, and without the West, where the sun goes down,' i.e. our love is subject neither to coldness nor to decline.

19–21] After considerable hesitation I have decided to adopt for ll. 20–1 the reading of a fair number of manuscripts, including some which may embody revisions by Donne himself. There are various alternative readings, the chief of which is that of the 1633 edition, adopted by Grierson:

> If our two loves be one, or, thou and I
> Love so alike, that none do slacken, none can die.

The disadvantages of that reading are, in my view, twofold: (1) The last line is insufficiently conclusive in point of rhythm; and, more important, (2) the sense involves confusion, for, on the one hand, there seems nothing to prevent two precisely similar loves both slackening to a precisely similar degree: while, on the other, if 'loving so alike' necessarily excluded that possibility, by precluding the possibility of slackening at all, then the mention of slackening would be redundant to the point of absurdity. I believe that the reading I have adopted, which avoids all these objections, may well have represented Donne's further thought on the matter. He may have *meant* by slackening, the relative slackening of one love as contrasted with the other: but he could easily have come to see that the words he used were susceptible of another, and confusing, interpretation.

The meaning of ll. 19–21 as printed in the present edition seems to me to be roughly this: 'Everything that dies contains some element of contrariety. If our two loves are either numerically one, or exactly similar in all respects, then neither of them can come to a end.'

I feel sure that Grierson was absolutely right in referring to the passage in the *Summa Theologica* (1, Qu. lxxv, Art. 6), in which St Thomas Aquinas says that corruption only occurs where there is contrariety. That passage seems to me to explain the words

> or, thou and I
> Love just alike in all, none of these loves can dic.

while the doctrine of the indestructibility of simple substances explains the assertion that if the lovers' loves be one, those loves cannot die. But some readers may still find difficulty in the word 'equally'. I think the point is that the word 'equally' here means 'uniformly' or 'consistently', so that every part of the mixture will be qualitatively the same as every other part. The term 'equally' would then be anticipating the second of the two alternatives that Donne suggests in ll. 20–1, viz. that the loves of himself and his mistress (or wife) should be entirely similar.

SONG

Go and catch a falling star,
  Get with child a mandrake root,
Tell me where all past years are,
  Or who cleft the Devil's foot,
Teach me to hear mermaids singing,
  Or to keep off envy's stinging,
      And find
      What wind
Serves to advance an honest mind.

If thou be'st borne to strange sights,
  Things invisible to see,
Ride ten thousand days and nights,
  Till age snow white hairs on thee,
Thou, when thou return'st, wilt tell me
  All strange wonders that befell thee,
      And swear
      Nowhere
Lives a woman true, and fair.

If thou findst one, let me know,
  Such a pilgrimage were sweet;—
Yet do not, I would not go,
  Though at next door we might meet;
Though she were true, when you met her,
  And last, till you write your letter,
      Yet she
      Will be
False, ere I come, to two, or three.

2 *Get with child a mandrake root*] i.e. beget a child on a fork-rooted plant. The forked root of *atropa mandragora* resembles the human form: sometimes the female form, sometimes the male, according to whether the roots are twofold or threefold. It is not the case that they all resemble the male form, and so I do not think there is the additional idea here of the impossibility of a male begetting a child on a male.

10] 'If you *are* strongly drawn to see strange sights.' (As Mr W. G. Ingram points out to me, the rhythm places the emphasis on 'be'st'.)

WOMAN'S CONSTANCY

Now thou hast lov'd me one whole day,
Tomorrow when thou leav'st, what wilt thou say?
Wilt thou then antedate some new-made vow?
        Or say that now
We are not just those persons which we were?
Or, that oaths made in reverential fear
Of Love, and his wrath, any may forswear?
Or, as true deaths true marriages untie,
So lovers' contracts, images of those,
Bind but till sleep, death's image, them unloose?
        Or, your own end to justify,
For having purpos'd change, and falsehood, you
Can have no way but falsehood to be true?
Vain lunatic, against these 'scapes I could
        Dispute, and conquer, if I would;
        Which I abstain to do,
For by tomorrow, I may think so too.

WOMAN'S CONSTANCY

2 *when thou leav'st*] when you stop loving me.

8 *true*] real.

14 *Vain*] ineffectual.
'scapes] subterfuges.

17 *I may think so too*] i.e. I may want to end our relationship too.

THE UNDERTAKING
or
PLATONIC LOVE

I have done one braver thing
  Than all the Worthies did,
And yet a braver thence doth spring,
  Which is, to keep that hid.

It were but madness now to impart
  The skill of specular stone,
When he which can have learn'd the art,
  To cut it, can find none.

So, if I now should utter this,
  Others (because no more
Such stuff to work upon there is)
  Would love but as before.

But he who loveliness within
  Hath found, all outward loathes,
For he who colour loves, and skin,
  Loves but their oldest clothes.

If, as I have, you also do
  Virtue attir'd in woman see,
And dare love that, and say so too,
  And forget the He and She;

And if this love, though placèd so,
  From profane men you hide,
Which will no faith on this bestow,
  Or, if they do, deride:

Then you have done a braver thing
  Than all the Worthies did;
And a braver thence will spring,
  Which is, to keep that hid.

THE UNDERTAKING or PLATONIC LOVE

Note on the title: In the 1633 edition and most of the MSS the poem bears no title. *The Undertaking* is the title given in the 1635–69 editions. *Platonic Love* is the title given in several MSS. I have preserved both titles, because I believe that to do so contributes to an understanding of the poem.

1 *braver*] finer, more glorious.

2 *all the Worthies*] The Nine Worthies were most usually understood to be three Gentiles, Hector, Alexander, and Julius Caesar; three Jews, Joshua, David, and Judas Maccabaeus; and three Christians, Arthur, Charlemagne, and Godfrey of Bouillon. As Dryden puts it in *The Flower and the Leaf*:

> Nine Worthies were they called, of different rites,
> Three Jews, three Pagans, and three Christian knights.

As Professor Grierson has pointed out, however, the list was variously made up, so that the term 'All the Worthies' would cover a wide field.

6 *the skill of specular stone*] A difficult phrase, which has caused trouble to commentators. I think the phrase most probably means 'the method of cutting old selenite': and that ll. 6–8 therefore mean: 'It would be absurd to teach anybody now how to cut old selenite into sheets, since anyone who might learn how to cut it, would not be able to find any to cut.' Old selenite was a stone apparently used in ancient times for glazing. It was prepared by being cut into thin sheets. In Donne's time there was a widespread belief that the stone was no longer available. Donne himself evidently believed this. He refers in other passages to the use of specular stone in ancient times for glazing, e.g. in a verse Letter to the Countess of Bedford (Grierson, I. 219), ll. 28–30:

> You teach (though wee learne not) a thing unknowne
> To our late times, the use of specular stone,
> Through which all things within without were shown.

and in Sermon 27 of *Fifty Sermons*: Alford, IV. 472–3: 'The heathens served their gods in temples, *sub dio*, without roofs or coverings, in a free openness; and, where they could, in temples made of specular-stone, that was transparent as glass, or crystal, so as they which walked without in the streets, might see all that was done within.' (A fuller account is included in Appendix II, p. 139.)

7–8] It is perhaps worth mentioning a point of punctuation here. The editions of 1633–54 print these lines:

> When he which can have learn'd the art,
> To cut it can find none.

The 1669 edition reads:

> When he, which can have learn'd the art
> To cut it, can find none.

This text was rightly preferred by Grierson. On the other hand there is a MS reading which is an improvement even on that of 1669. It is, e.g., the reading of the Camb. Univ. Lib. Add. MS 5778, and is that adopted in the present text. This MS reading may account for the comma in 1633, but whatever its bibliographical status, it makes for the sense of the poem. It brings out most clearly that 'the art', i.e. 'the skill of specular stone,' is the art of *cutting* specular stone.

9–12] 'In the same way, if I should tell anyone about this Platonic love of mine, since there is no woman left who can be loved in just this way, it would make no difference to other people's ways of loving; they would go on loving in the same way as they did before.'

16 *Loves but their oldest clothes*] 'loves merely the oldest clothes of the women he purports to love, as opposed to their real selves.' (The 'oldest clothes' might mean either the bodies of individual women, or the physical characteristics of women since Eve.)

20] i.e. and forget sex.

21–2] i.e. And if you hide this love, which you have set upon the Platonic idea of virtue, from the common run of people, who cannot understand such mysteries.

23] 'who will not believe this to be true.'

25] with the implication, of course, that this is what Donne himself has done.

THE SUN RISING

It is possible that the idea of this poem was suggested to Donne by Ovid, *Amores*, I. 13: but if it was, Donne has made many startlingly original departures.

It is noteworthy that the thought of the latter half of stanza 2 strongly resembles that of parts of stanzas 2 and 3 of *The Anniversarie*.

7] Mr Leishman, in *The Monarch of Wit*, suggests that this line is probably evidence that the poem was written in 1603 or after.

8 *offices*] tasks.

9 *Love, all alike*] love, which is unchanging.

10 *the rags of time*] the mere tattered clothing of time: or alternatively, the shreds into which time is torn up and subdivided. Mr John Hayward, in the Nonesuch Donne, refers to *LXXX Sermons*, II. 12–13. That is a passage in which Donne, speaking of mercy, says: 'the names of first or last derogate from it, for first and last are but rags of time, and his mercy hath no relation to time, no limitation to time, it is not first nor last, but eternal, everlasting.'

17 *both the Indias of spice and mine*] the East Indies and the West Indies respectively. Cf. a letter from Donne to Sir Robert Carr (1624?): 'Your way into *Spain* was Eastward, and that is the way to the land of Perfumes and Spices; their way hither is Westward, and that is the way to the land of Gold, and of Mynes.'

21] 'she is all the states there are, and I am all the princes there are.'

24 *alchemy*] mere counterfeit.

30] 'this bed is the centre of your orbit, and these walls mark your orbit itself.'

THE SUN RISING

Busy old fool, unruly Sun,
Why dost thou thus,
Through windows, and through curtains, call on us?
Must to thy motions lovers' seasons run?
Saucy pedantic wretch, go chide
Late schoolboys, and sour prentices,
Go tell court-huntsmen that the King will ride,
Call country ants to harvest offices;
Love, all alike, no season knows, nor clime,
Nor hours, days, months, which are the rags of time.

Thy beams, so reverend and strong
Why shouldst thou think?
I could eclipse and cloud them with a wink,
But that I would not lose her sight so long:
If her eyes have not blinded thine,
Look, and tomorrow late, tell me
Whether both the Indias of spice and mine
Be where thou leftst them, or lie here with me.
Ask for those Kings whom thou saw'st yesterday,
And thou shalt hear: 'All here in one bed lay.'

She is[1] all States, and all Princes I,
Nothing else is:
Princes do but play us; compar'd to this,
All honour's mimic, all wealth alchemy.
Thou, sun, art half as happy as we,
In that the world's contracted thus;
Thine age asks ease, and since thy duties be
To warm the world, that's done in warming us.
Shine here to us, and thou art everywhere;
This bed thy centre is, these walls, thy sphere.

1. For the significance of the slur in the present recension see note on p. li.

THE INDIFFERENT

I can love both fair and brown,
Her whom abundance melts, and her whom want betrays,
Her who loves loneness best, and her who masks and plays,
Her whom the country form'd, and whom the town,
Her who believes, and her who tries,
Her who still weeps with spongy eyes,
And her who is dry cork, and never cries;
I can love her, and her, and you, and you,
I can love any, so she be not true.

Will no other vice content you?
Will it not serve your turn to do as did your mothers?
Or have you all old vices spent, and now would find out others?
Or doth a fear, that men are true, torment you?
Oh we are not, be not you so.
Let me, and do you, twenty know.
Rob me, but bind me not, and let me go.
Must I, who came to travel thorough you,
Grow your fix'd subject, because you are true?

Venus heard me sigh this song,
And by love's sweetest part, variety, she swore
She heard not this till now; and that it should be so no more.
She went, examin'd, and return'd ere long,
And said: 'Alas, some two or three
Poor heretics in love there be,
Which think to stablish dangerous constancy.
But I have told them: "Since you will be true,
You shall be true to them, who are false to you!" '

THE INDIFFERENT

1 *brown*] i.e. not merely the conventional Elizabethan beauty, who was fair.

2] the woman who is made amorous by living in luxury, and the woman who gives herself because she needs money.

5] the woman who trusts her lover, and the woman who tests him.

10 *no other vice*] i.e. than being true!

11 *to do as did your mothers*] i.e. to be promiscuous (the word 'do' may even have a strong sexual sense).

17 *travel*] The original spelling 'travail' suggests more strongly a possible *double entendre*.
thorough] through.

22 *examin'd*] like an inquisitor.

25] 'who are planning' (or 'who fancy they may manage') 'to establish the dangerous doctrine of constancy'.

26] It is perhaps worth mentioning that one of the good MSS which has come to light since Professor Grierson's 1912 edition (Camb. Univ. Lib. Add. MS 5778) reads:

> But I have tolld them since they will be true,
> Yo^{u} shall be true to them, who were false to yo^{u}.

will be] insist on being.

LOVE'S USURY

For every hour that thou wilt spare me now,
I will allow,
Usurious God of Love, twenty to thee,
When with my brown, my gray hairs equal be;
Till then, Love, let my body reign, and let
Me travel, sojourn, snatch, plot, have, forget,
Resume my last year's relict: think that yet
We'd never met.

Let me think any rival's letter mine,
And at next nine
Keep midnight's promise; mistake by the way
The maid, and tell the lady of that delay;
Only let me love none, no, not the sport;
From country grass, to comfitures of Court,
Or city's quelque-choses, let report
My mind transport.

This bargain's good; if, when I'm old, I be
Inflam'd by thee,
If thine own honour, or my shame, or pain,
Thou covet, most at that age thou shalt gain.
Do thy will then, then subject and degree
And fruit of love, Love, I submit to thee;
Spare me till then, I'll bear it, though she be
One that loves me.

LOVE'S USURY

5 *let my body reign*] 'let physical passion rule me.'

6 *snatch*] seize opportunities of physical gratification.

7–8] 'take up again the woman I cast off last year, and imagine we had never met before.'

11–12] *mistake by the way the maid*] meaning (1) take the maid to be the lady, and (2) seduce the maid.

9–12] 'Let me take any letter addressed to a rival to be addressed to me, and let me be quite irresponsible about turning up in time for a midnight assignation, and arrive at nine next morning, through having taken the maid for the lady (seduced the maid), and let me be impudent enough to tell the lady that this was the cause of the delay.'

13 *no, not the sport*] 'let me not even fall in love with the physical play itself.' This may be taken either generally, or, as is the view of Mr Edward Gillott, of King's College, with whom I have discussed this passage, as referring to the pleasure of sexuality with any *particular* woman. The latter interpretation seems to me the better.

14–16] possibly Donne is here using 'grass', 'comfitures', and 'quelque-choses' figuratively, for the various types of women on his large playground.

14 *comfitures*] literally 'sweetmeats'.

15 *quelque-choses*] (*choses* disyllabic) literally 'dainties', 'fancy trifles', another spelling of 'kickshaws'. In a letter to Sir Henry Goodyer (1609 ?) Donne writes, referring to some aphoristic observations in the letter: 'These, Sir, are the salads and onions of *Mitcham*, sent to you with as wholesome affection as your other friends send Melons and Quelque-choses from Court and London.' Of the application of the term 'Quelque-choses' to *persons*, there are other instances in seventeenth-century literature (see *O.E.D.*).

15–16 *let . . . transport*] 'let information as to the women to be found in these localities switch my attention from one to another.'

17 *This bargain's good*] i.e. from the point of view of Love the usurer.

20] This is the reading of one good MS (Camb. Univ. Lib. Add. MS 5778) which has come to light since Grierson's 1912 edition. The early printed editions, followed by Grierson, place the comma after 'most'. The MS reading I have adopted seems to me to make much better sense. I see that it was proposed by Mr John Sparrow to Mr John Hayward as an emendation, and adopted by the latter in the Nonesuch Donne. Mr Hayward also points out that it was the reading of the Leconfield MS, another good MS, now in the library of Sir Geoffrey Keynes. I find that it is also the reading of *L74* and of *Lut*.

21–2] 'when that time comes, do exactly what you like with me: I will abide then by what you lay down as to whom I shall love, how much I shall love, and what the fruit of my love shall be.'

22 *fruit*] possibly 'result', possibly 'offspring', possibly both.

23–4 *though she be . . . me*] cynical indeed: when that time arrives (but not now), Donne will even stand loving someone who is in love with him.

THE CANONIZATION

For God's sake hold your tongue, and let me love,
Or chide my palsy, or my gout,
My five gray hairs, or ruin'd fortune flout,
With wealth your state, your mind with arts improve,
Take you a course, get you a place,
Observe his honour, or his grace,
Or the King's real, or his stampèd face
Contemplate; what you will, approve,
So you will let me love.

Alas, alas, who's injured by my love?
What merchant's ships have my sighs drown'd?
Who says my tears have overflow'd his ground?
When did my colds a forward spring remove?
When did the heats which my veins fill
Add one man to the plaguy bill?
Soldiers find wars, and lawyers find out still
Litigious men, which quarrels move,
Though she and I do love.

Call us what you will, we are made such by love;
Call her one, me another fly,
We are tapers too, and at our own cost die,
And we in us find the Eagle and the Dove.
The Phoenix riddle hath more wit
By us; we two being one, are it.
So to one neutral thing both sexes fit,

We die and rise the same, and prove
Mysterious by this love.

We can die by it, if not live by love,
And if unfit for tombs and hearse
Our legend be, it will be fit for verse;
And if no piece of chronicle we prove,

THE CANONIZATION

2 *Or . . . or*] Either . . . or.

5 *Take you a course*] This might possibly have the same meaning as now: 'take a course', of philosophy, mathematics, or whatever it might be: but I think that it is much more probable that it means 'settle down to a career'. The word 'course' is used as equivalent to 'career' in a letter from Donne to Sir Henry Goodyer (1609 ?). *O.E.D.* gives Elizabethan authority for both meanings.

get you a place] get a job or post for yourself.

6 *Observe*] 'be attentive to' (and therefore, probably 'pay court to', a sense in which the term was used as late as 1754 by Richardson in *Sir Charles Grandison*: 'Clementina loves to be punctiliously observed.' (See *O.E.D.*)).

7] i.e. frequent the Court, or go in for money-making.

8 *approve*] 'experience', 'try', an obsolete sense of the term (see *O.E.D.*).

9 *so*] if only.

13] thereby damaging the farmers.

14–15] there may be an implication here that in such a case the playhouses would have been forced to close.

15 *man*] I have ventured to adopt this more vivid reading of the overwhelming number of the known MSS and of the 1669 edition, in preference to the reading 'more' of the 1633–54 editions, which is followed, though somewhat reluctantly, by Grierson.

plaguy bill] bill of mortality from the plague. Professor Garrod, in his note on the line in *Donne: Poetry and Prose* (Clarendon Press, 1946), p. 111, says these bills were probably issued weekly, and points out that printed bills probably began to be issued in 1592. He thinks Donne's reference is probably to the plague of 1592–3: but surely that would not accord with the mention of the King in l. 7 ? 1603 seems a reasonable alternative.

17 *which quarrels move*] who stir up quarrels.

20 *fly*] probably because they seem to be wheeling aimlessly round each other (suggesting naturally the succeeding image of the tapers). Cf. Donne's Elegy VI, ll. 17–19:

> so, the taper's beamy eye
> Amorously twinkling beckons the giddy fly,
> Yet burns his wings; . . .

21 *We‿are*] The slur helps to indicate that the emphasis is to be placed not on 'we' but on 'tapers too'.

21] 'Each of us is a taper, as well as a fly, and each of us is therefore burnt by the other, but the one who kills kills at his or her own cost,' for the tapers are themselves diminishing. I owe this suggestion to Professor Grierson, in discussion. If the explanation is correct, I think it is not impossible that there is also here a reference to the popular belief that the act of love diminishes length of life (cf. *Farewell to Love*, ll. 28–30). The word 'die' was commonly used in Elizabethan slang to refer to sexual detumescence.

We'll build in sonnets pretty rooms;
As well a well-wrought urn becomes
The greatest ashes, as half-acre tombs,
And by these hymns, all shall approve
Us *canoniz'd* for Love:

And thus invoke us: 'You, whom reverend love
Made one another's hermitage;
You, to whom love was peace, that now is rage;
Who did the whole world's soul contract, and drove
Into the glasses of your eyes
(So made such mirrors, and such spies,
That they did all to you epitomize)
Countries, towns, courts: beg from above
A pattern of your love!'

22] 'We find *in each other* the most tyrannical and the gentlest of beings, and so we prey on each other.' The Eagle and the Dove were almost proverbially the types of the predatory and the meek: cf. Ovid, *Ars Amatoria*, I. 117:

> Ut fugiunt aquilas timidissima turba columbae
> As timid doves from the fierce eagle fly
> (tr. Wolferston (1661)).

Cf. also in the work of writers contemporary with Donne:

> If you have writ your annals true, 'tis there,
> That, like an eagle in a dove-cote, I
> Flutter'd your Volscians in Corioli...
> (*Coriolanus*, V. v. 114–16)

and

> But who does hawk at eagles with a dove?
> (G. Herbert, *The Sacrifice*, xxiii).

23–7] 'The riddle of the Phoenix' (viz. how it perpetuates its species, though there is never more than one in existence at a time) 'makes more sense because of us; for we two, being one, are the Phoenix. Our two sexes fit together so perfectly to form a being of no sex, that after we die we come to life again the same being that we were before, just as the identical Phoenix rises from its own ashes; and this love makes us a mystery worthy of reverence.'

26 *die*] commonly used in Elizabethan slang for sexual expiration (cf. note on l. 21).

32 *sonnets pretty rooms*] Mr James Reeves (*Donne, Selected Poems*, Heinemann, 1953) points out that there is a clever conceit here. Donne is using 'sonnets' loosely for a love poem, and *stanza* in Italian means a room.

33 *becomes*] 'suits', 'befits'.

35 *approve*] 'prove' or 'confirm'.

37–45] Grierson has, in my view, thoroughly cleared up the text of this stanza. For my modern recension I have only added inverted commas in ll. 37 and 45, a mere matter of change of convention.

40–4 *and drove into the glasses of your eyes . . . Countries, towns, courts*] i.e. made yourselves self-sufficient in knowledge of the world, since everything in the world is to be found in each of you, for you are each a world. The sense of 'drove' would, I think, be closely rendered in modern English by 'crammed'.

44–5 *beg from above A pattern of your love*] i.e. 'ask God to give us a pattern of your love, so that others may love as you did.' They are now saints (cf. l. 36), and, as Professor Grierson has suggested to me, it is perhaps worth mentioning that this request conforms to the Roman Catholic doctrine that men pray to saints to pray for them.

THE TRIPLE FOOL

I am two fools, I know,
For loving, and for saying so
In whining poetry;
But where's that wiseman, that would not be I,
If she would not deny?
Then, as the earth's inward narrow crooked lanes
Do purge sea-water's fretful salt away,
I thought, if I could draw my pains
Through rhyme's vexation, I should them allay:
Grief brought to numbers cannot be so fierce;
For he tames it, that fetters it in verse.

But when I have done so,
Some man, his art and voice to show,
Doth set and sing my pain,
And, by delighting many, frees again
Grief, which verse did restrain.
To love and grief tribute of verse belongs,
But not of such as pleases when 'tis read;
Both are increasèd by such songs:
For both their triumphs so are publishèd,
And I, which was two fools, do so grow three;
Who are a little wise, the best fools be.

THE TRIPLE FOOL

As Grierson says in his note (II. 17): The poet is trebly a fool because (1) he loves, (2) he expresses his love in verse, (3) he thereby enables someone to set the verse to music and by singing it to re-awaken the passion which poetical composition had lulled to sleep.

4 *wiseman*] meaning both (1) something similar to the modern American 'wise guy', or to the still current English word 'wiseacre' (cf. Mr Worldly Wiseman in *Pilgrim's Progress*), and (2) wise man. Donne uses the single word in sense (2) elsewhere, e.g. in a passage in one of the Sermons (ed. Potter and Simpson, VI. 99).

6 *Then*] 'thus', 'so'; alternatively 'then (when I berhymed my lady)'.

14 *set*] set to music.

LOVERS' INFINITENESS

If yet I have not all thy love,
Dear, I shall never have it all;
I cannot breathe one other sigh, to move,
Nor can intreat one other tear to fall;
And all my treasure, which should purchase thee—
Sighs, tears, and oaths, and letters—I have spent;
Yet no more can be due to me,
Than at the bargain made was meant;
If then thy gift of love were partial,
That some to me, some should to others fall,
  Dear, I shall never have thee all.

Or if then thou gavest me all,
All was but all which thou hadst then;
But if in thy heart, since, there be or shall
New love created be, by other men,
Which have their stocks entire, and can in tears,
In sighs, in oaths, in letters, outbid me,
This new love may beget new fears,
For this love was not vowed by thee:
And yet it was, thy gift being general;
The ground, thy heart, is mine; whatever shall
  Grow there, dear, I should have it all.

Yet I would not have all yet,
He that hath all can have no more,
And since my love doth every day admit
New growth, thou shouldst have new rewards in store;
Thou canst not every day give me thy heart;
If thou canst give it, then thou never gavest it:
Love's riddles are, that though thy heart depart,
It stays at home, and thou with losing savest it:
But we will have a way more liberal
Than changing hearts, to join them, so we shall
  Be one, and one another's All.

LOVERS' INFINITENESS

Note on the title: Grierson comments that this title, which appears only in the printed editions, is a strange one, but it would seem to me to fit the sense of the poem. The poet is capable of giving more and more love each day (l. 25), and his lady ought to be able to give ever fresh rewards. This would only be possible if the lovers were themselves infinite.

9 *partial*] trisyllabic word.

14–15] But if new love has since been created in your heart, or will be created there some time, by other men.

18] This new love may cause me fresh anxiety.

29 *Love's riddles are*] The paradoxical facts about love are . . .

SONG

Sweetest love, I do not go for weariness of thee,
Nor in hope the world can show a fitter love for me;
But since that I
Must die at last, 'tis best
To use myself in jest,
Thus by feign'd deaths to die;

Yesternight the Sun went hence, and yet is here today;
He hath no desire nor sense, nor half so short a way:
Then fear not me,
But believe that I shall make
Speedier journeys, since I take
More wings and spurs than he.

Oh how feeble is man's power; that if good fortune fall,
Cannot add another hour, nor a lost hour recall!
But come bad chance,
And we join to it our strength,
And we teach it art and length,
Itself o'er us to advance.

When thou sigh'st, thou sigh'st not wind, but sigh'st my soul away,
When thou weep'st, unkindly kind, my life's blood doth decay.
It cannot be
That thou lov'st me, as thou say'st,
If in thine my life thou waste;
Thou art the best of me.

Let not thy divining heart forethink me any ill;
Destiny may take thy part, and may thy fears fulfil;
But think that we
Are but turn'd aside to sleep;
They who one another keep
Alive, ne'er parted be.

SONG

General Note: I have adopted the layout to be found in some of the MSS, where what appear in the printed editions as the first four lines of each stanza are written as two long lines. This seems to me to reveal a formal beauty of contrast within each stanza, which is not apparent in the usual method of printing the poem, which follows the old printed editions. In some manuscripts, for instance *C57*, *TCC*, and *Lut*, ll. 4 and 5 in the present text (and the corresponding lines in later stanzas) are also written as one long line: but this is not done in all the MSS, e.g. Camb. Univ. Lib. Add. MS 29D (Grierson: *C*) writes these two lines separately. I have hesitated between the two types of layout for these lines, but finally decided to print them as in each case two separate lines, partly to emphasize the consecutive rhyme.

5–6] to accustom myself to death by playing at it.

17 *length*] probably meaning either how to expand or stretch, or 'how to range on us'. (There is an obsolete sense of the word 'length', which is equivalent to the still current gunnery term 'range' (see *O.E.D.*). Cf. the similar use in cricket.)

20 *unkindly kind*] either (1) 'malignantly kind person', meaning that by weeping she is showing her kindness to him in a way which is in fact malignant; or (2) 'unnaturally kind person', the force of the expression then being, as Mr Ingram has suggested to me, that the general run of women are naturally unkind. 'Unkindly' had at the time a stronger negative force than 'unkind' today.

25 *divining*] prophetic (with the sense of foreboding and uncanny guessing).

THE LEGACY

When I died last (and, dear, I die
  As often as from thee I go),
  Though it be but an hour ago,
And lovers' hours be full eternity,
I can remember yet, that I
  Something did say, and something did bestow;
Though I be dead, which sent me, I should be
Mine own executor and legacy.

I heard me say: 'Tell her anon,
  That my self' (that is you, not I)
  'Did kill me'; and when I felt me die,
I bid me send my heart, when I was gone;
But I alas could there find none,
  When I had ripp'd me, and search'd where hearts did lie;
It kill'd me again, that I who still was true
In life, in my last will should cozen you.

Yet I found something like a heart,
  But colours it, and corners had;
  It was not good, it was not bad,
It was entire to none, and few had part.
As good as could be made by art
  It seem'd; and therefore, for our losses sad,
I meant to send this heart instead of mine:
But oh, no man could hold it, for 'twas thine.

THE LEGACY

1–5] A difficult passage, which has been variously punctuated in the modern editions. I follow Grierson, except that I have inserted a parenthesis from 'and' to 'go', to try to make the sense clearer. The sense seems to me to be: 'When I died last (and, dear, I die every time I leave you), even though it was just an hour ago, and lovers' hours are each a whole eternity, I can still remember that . . .'

3 *but*] *not* 'only', which would make nonsense, but 'just' (cf. 'but now' = 'just now'). The word may have already caused difficulty in the seventeenth century: it is omitted in some MSS (e.g. *A25*, *H40*, *Lut*, *SP*).

7–8] I think this probably means: 'Though I, who sent myself, am dead, I was to be my own executor and my own legacy.'

9–16] A stanza which has caused great difficulty. My own reading agrees partly with Chambers and partly with Grierson. I entirely concur with Grierson against Norton and Chambers that the stop at the end of l. 14 should be heavier than that at the end of l. 13, and that ll. 15 and 16 are a comment on the whole incident. On the other hand, I believe Chambers was right against Grierson in ending the inverted commas after 'me' in l. 11. The sense seems to me to be: 'I heard myself say: "Tell her presently that it was my self" (my self being you not me) "that killed me"; and then when I felt myself dying I told myself to send you my heart when I was dead; but when I ripped my body open, and looked in the place where hearts used to be located, I failed to find one there; and the thought that I, who was always true to you during life, should cheat you in my will, killed me all over again.'

18 *colours*] probably meaning that it was a painted heart, i.e. a hypocritical one, not a 'true plain' one. This heart was, of course, that of his mistress (cf. l. 24).
corners] The circle and sphere were considered to be the most perfect forms. In *Fifty Sermons*, XXVII. I, Donne says: 'God hath made all things in a *Roundnesse* . . . God hath wrapped up all things in Circles, and then a Circle hath no *Angles*; there are no *Corners* in a Circle.'

20 *It was entire to none*] It was not given wholly to anyone.
and few had part] and few had a share in its affections.

22 *for our losses sad*] 'being sad for our losses'; probably, that is, for his loss of his heart and her loss of him and his heart.

24] 'I could not send it, for no one could hold such a fickle heart as yours.'

A FEVER

Oh do not die, for I shall hate
  All women so, when thou art gone,
That thee I shall not celebrate,
  When I remember, thou wast one.

But yet thou canst not die, I know;
  To leave this world behind, is death;
But when thou from this world wilt go,
  The whole world vapours with thy breath.

Or if, when thou, the world's soul, goest,
  It stay, 'tis but thy carcase then;
The fairest woman, but thy ghost,
  But corrupt worms, the worthiest men.

O wrangling schools, that search what fire
  Shall burn this world, had none the wit
Unto this knowledge to aspire,
  That this her fever might be it?

And yet she cannot waste by this,
  Nor long bear this torturing wrong,
For much corruption needful is,
  To fuel such a fever long.

These burning fits but meteors be,
  Whose matter in thee is soon spent:
Thy beauty, and all parts which are thee,
  Are unchangeable firmament.

Yet 'twas of my mind, seizing thee,
  Though it in thee cannot persévér:
For I had rather owner be
  Of thee one hour, than all else ever.

A FEVER

5–8] But yet actually I know that you can't die; for death consists in leaving this world behind; but you can't leave this world behind, because when you depart, the world will evaporate in your last breath.

11–12] The most beautiful woman will be merely a ghost of you, and the finest men nothing but corrupt worms.

13–14 *O wrangling schools . . . world*] The Stoics taught that the physical world would, at the end of each cycle of existence, be destroyed by a general conflagration. This gave rise to the question what fire would give rise to the general conflagration. Most Stoics thought the destroying fire was primary fire or ether. Cleanthes, however, thought that the source of destruction would be the sun. (See Zeller, *Stoics, Epicureans and Sceptics*, tr. Reichel, Longmans, ed. 1892, pp. 161–9.) In the Early Christian era, probably partly under Stoic influence, a fair number of writers, both Gnostic (e.g. Valentinus) and Patristic (e.g. Irenaeus, Hippolytus and Origen), as well as Manichaean, put forward the idea of a world-consuming fire, describing and disputing about its origin and nature.

14–15 *had none the wit . . . aspire*] didn't anyone have the intelligence to catch a glimpse of the possibility . . . ?

19–20] There would have to be much corruption in her to keep such a fever going for long (and there is not).

21–2] i.e. these feverish fits are nothing but the heat of foreign bodies, which will soon be dissolved in you.

24] i.e. are as unchangeable as the sphere of the fixed stars.

25] 'Yet it had the same idea as I have, in seizing you.' There is a legal quibble here. 'To seize' meant also to take corporeal possession of something as owner. This gives added significance to the word 'owner' in l. 27.

26 *persével*] persist.

28 *than all else ever*] i.e. than owner in perpetuity of everything else in the world.

AIR AND ANGELS

Twice or thrice had I loved thee,
Before I knew thy face or name;
So in a voice, so in a shapeless flame
Angels affect us oft, and worshipp'd be;
Still when, to where thou wert, I came,
Some lovely glorious nothing I did see:
But since my soul, whose child love is,
Takes limbs of flesh, and else could nothing do,
More subtle than the parent is
Love must not be, but take a body too;
And therefore what thou wert, and who,
I bid Love ask, and now
That it assume thy body, I allow,
And fix itself in thy lip, eye, and brow.

Whilst thus to ballast love I thought,
And so more steadily to have gone,
With wares which would sink admiration
I saw I had love's pinnace overfraught;
Every thy hair for love to work upon
Is much too much, some fitter must be sought;
For, nor in nothing, nor in things
Extreme, and scattering bright, can love inhere:
Then, as an Angel, face, and wings
Of air, not pure as it, yet pure, doth wear,
So thy love may be my love's sphere;
Just such disparity
As is 'twixt Air and Angels' purity,
'Twixt women's love, and men's, will ever be.

AIR AND ANGELS

General Note: As this poem is notoriously one of the most difficult of the *Songs and Sonets*, I think it is perhaps best to start by giving a close paraphrase of the whole poem, as I interpret it; and then to try to justify controversial points in notes on particular lines and passages.

The sense of the poem seems to me to be as follows:

'I had loved the idea of you two or three times, as incompletely manifested in other women, before I actually met *you*. (Angels often affect us in a similar way. They appear in a voice or a formless flame, and we worship them in that guise.) Moreover, every time I came to the place where you were so manifested, what I saw was some beautiful and splendid, but quite indeterminate thing. But [I thought that] since my soul has taken on a body, and would be useless without it, my love, which is my soul's child, ought not to be more ethereal than its parent, but should also assume a body: and so I told my love to enquire what sort of a person and who you were, and then gave it permission to assume your body, and take up its permanent abode in your face.

'I intended in this way to keep my skimming craft of love steady, by ballasting her, but I saw to my horror that I had not merely ballasted the little ship, but overloaded her with wares which would sink even admiration'; (then the metaphor suddenly changes) 'even a single hair of yours presents too great a task for love to work upon it. I must look for some more suitable body for my love than your physical body. For love cannot inhere either in nothing or in things which are too concentrated and destructively brilliant. So the solution must be that just as an angel (to appear to human beings) takes on a face and wings of air (not as pure as the angel itself, of course, but pure all the same), so my love must assume your *love* as its body, or, to vary the metaphor, my love must take your love as its sphere, just as an angel moves in and exerts control over a sphere [or, if we take 'sphere' to mean *element*, 'so my love must assume your love as the body or element in which it can act']. As a matter of fact, the perennial difference between male and female love *is* that women's love, though pure like air, is not quite so pure as men's love, which is as pure as an angel.'

1–2] cf. *The Good-morrow* (l. 7): 'a dream of thee'; cf. also Hardy's *The Well-Beloved*, as Professor Grierson has suggested to me.

3] i.e. manifested very incompletely and temporarily.

3–4] It appears from the interesting researches of Miss Mary Paton Ramsay (*Les Doctrines Médiévales chez Donne*, Oxford, 1917, 2nd edn, 1924), that Donne fairly certainly accepted the view that angels are immaterial. This view had to face the problem how such immaterial beings could communicate with men. To solve it certain Christian philosophers, including Dionysius the Areopagite and, later, St Thomas Aquinas, had adapted a neo-Platonic doctrine found in Plotinus. That doctrine concerned the human soul, and it was that the human soul, when it descends into the world, first joins itself to an ethereal body, viz. 'spirit' (πνεῦμα), which acts as its vehicle. Plotinus did not clarify this view: but his disciples Porphyry and Jamblichus did. The notion descended to the seventeenth-century philosopher, Cudworth. Dionysius and St Thomas did not hold this view about the human soul: but they did hold a somewhat analogous view about angels, namely, that they might take more or less rarefied bodies, in order to communicate with and influence men. Miss Ramsay herself thinks that this is the view that Donne is putting forward in these lines. I am not convinced that this is so. I certainly think Donne is probably alluding to this Thomist doctrine in the latter part of stanza 2: but in ll. 3–4, it seems to me, he might at least equally well be alluding to the view held by Moses Maimonides, whose work he also knew, that angels only *appear* to have bodies, e.g. flames or human bodies (see *Guide des Egarés*, I. ch. xlix). St Thomas Aquinas, in the passage from the *Summa Theologica* (I. li. 2) quoted by Grierson (II. 21), writes that angels cannot assume bodies of fire, for if they did they would burn everything they touched. In that case it would not seem that it could consistently be Thomist doctrine that an angel should really appear in a flame.

5] alternatively to my suggestion in the General Note, this line might mean: 'When I came into your *actual* presence, now as before, . . .'

15–16] I think these lines mean that Donne thought by this means to keep his love steady instead of flighty.

15–18] I believe that the subtlety of these lines is not generally appreciated. Donne had, I think, a sharp distinction in his mind between what we should call 'capsizing', and 'sinking without capsizing'. He puts the distinction in his own terminology in a letter to his friend Sir Henry Goodyer (possibly dated 1608). (This letter is reprinted in the *Nonesuch Donne*, p. 450). The relevant passage is as follows: 'The pleasantnesse of the season displeases me. Every thing refreshes, and I wither, and I grow older and not better, my strength diminishes, and my load growes, and being to passe more and more stormes, I finde that I have not only cast out all my ballast which nature and time gives, Reason and discretion, and so am as empty and light as Vanity can make me; but I have over fraught myself with Vice, and so am riddingly subject to two contrary wrackes, Sinking and Oversetting, . . .'

'Sinking', then, i.e. sinking through too great a cargo, is distinguished from 'Oversetting', i.e. capsizing through lack of ballast. Donne wanted to keep his little ship of love steady, to prevent it from *capsizing*: but he found he had gone to the opposite extreme, overloaded it, and so exposed it to the 'contrary wracke', *sinking*. He had thought he was simply ballasting the pinnace; he had loaded it with more than a full cargo. There is another parallel passage in the *Second Anniversarie*, where Donne writes about Elizabeth Drury (ll. 316–17):

(For so much knowledge, as would over-fraight
Another, did but ballast her).

17 *admiration*] pronounced as five syllables.

18 *pinnace*] a small light craft, sometimes used for reconnaissance, and I

think that is relevant here. Donne himself uses the word 'pinnace' with that force in a letter to Mrs Herbert (11 June 1607) in which he calls the letter itself 'a Pinnace to discover'.

24 *it*] The vexed point here is whether 'it' refers back to 'Angel' (l. 23) or to 'air' (l. 24). There are arguments in favour of each interpretation. (See Appendix III, p. 140.) My own view is that it definitely refers back to 'Angel'. If, however, it be taken to refer to 'air', then the reference is, in my view, merely parenthetical, and does not affect the point of the last three lines of the poem, namely, that women's love, though pure as air, is not quite as pure as men's love, which is as pure as an angel.

25 *sphere*] For the two possible meanings here see the General Note (above).

26–8] The controversy about these lines is as to whether they imply that women's love is purer than men's, or that men's love is purer than women's. My own view is that the implication is almost certainly that men's love is purer than women's. (For my arguments in favour of this view, see Appendix III, p. 142.)

BREAK OF DAY

'Tis true, 'tis day,—what though it be ?
Oh wilt thou therefore rise from me ?
Why should we rise because 'tis light ?
Did we lie down because 'twas night ?
Love, which in spite of darkness brought us hither,
Should in despite of light hold us together.

Light hath no tongue, but is all eye;
If it could speak as well as spy,
This is the worst that it could say,
That, being well, I fain would stay,
And that I love my heart and honour so,
That I would not from him, that hath them, go.

Must business thee from hence remove ?
Oh, that's the worst disease of love;
The poor, the foul, the false, love can
Admit, but not the busied man.
He which hath business, and makes love, doth do
Such wrong, as if a married man should woo.

BREAK OF DAY

General Note: It is important to realize at the outset that this poem is put into the mouth of the woman.

6 *hold*] I have adopted this stronger reading in preference to the usual 'keep', on the authority of a number of MSS, including some which may embody corrections by Donne himself.

9–12] I have ventured to adopt the present tenses: 'is' (l. 9), 'love' (l. 11), and 'hath' (l. 12), again with the support of a number of MSS, including some which may embody corrections by Donne himself. This reading seems to me to give greater vividness. It also seems to give something like a double effect to the stanza, i.e. this is what she *would* say in the hypothetical circumstances, but it is also what she is *in fact* saying now.

18] I have adopted the present reading on the authority of almost identical MSS to those mentioned in the note to ll. 9–12, in preference to the reading:

Such wrong, as when a married man doth woo,

which is the reading of the 1633 and 1669 editions, and of a number of other MSS, and is also the reading adopted by Grierson. My preference is slight, but is based mainly on the two following considerations: (1) the present reading avoids the repetition of 'doth'; (2) the present reading makes the end of the poem sharper, more cynical, than the other reading would. In addition, it is more consistent with the readings I have adopted elsewhere in the poem to follow these MSS here. It may be worth noting that the 1635–54 editions fall between two stools, by reading:

as when a married man should woo.

THE ANNIVERSARY

All Kings, and all their favourites,
All glory of honours, beauties, wits,
The Sun itself, which makes times, as they pass,
Is elder by a year, now, than it was
When thou and I first one another saw:
All other things to their destruction draw,
Only our love hath no decay;
This, no tomorrow hath, nor yesterday;
Running it never runs from us away,
But truly keeps his first, last, everlasting day.

Two graves must hide thine and my corse;
If one might, death were no divorce:
Alas, as well as other Princes, we
(Who Prince enough in one another be)
Must leave at last in death, these eyes, and ears,
Oft fed with true oaths, and with sweet salt tears;
But souls where nothing dwells but love
(All other thoughts being inmates) then shall prove
This, or a love increasèd there above,
When bodies to their graves, souls from their graves remove.

And then we shall be throughly blest,
But we no more than all the rest;
Here upon earth, we are Kings, and none but we
Can be such Kings, nor of such subjects be:
Who is so safe as we, where none can do
Treason to us, except one of us two?
True and false fears let us refrain,
Let us love nobly, and live, and add again
Years and years unto years, till we attain
To write threescore; this is the second of our reign.

THE ANNIVERSARY

3 *which makes times*] which makes the hours, days, years, and so on.

3] A difficult line. 'As they pass' is somewhat obscure. There are, I think, at least two possible ways of taking 'they': (1) to refer to 'times'; (2) to refer to the Kings and favourites, and the glory of honours, beauties, and wits. This ambiguity seems to have caused trouble already in the seventeenth century. The MSS and the 1633 edition read as here; but in the very next edition (1635), the reading is:

The Sun it selfe, which makes times, as these passe, . . .

'these' probably referring to 'times', as the last-mentioned word (cf. Lat. *hic*, as opposed to *ille*). This reading was retained up till the 1654 edition; but the 1669 edition reverted to the reading of the MSS and the 1633 edition. Unfortunately we cannot tell for certain what made the 1635 editor or editors change 'they' into 'these': or what made the 1669 editor revert to the original reading. On the whole, however, I should think that the most probable explanation is that the 1635 editor considered that the correct interpretation of 'they' was that it referred to the 'times', and that he wished to eliminate any suggestion that 'they' might refer to the Kings, and so on (we have no evidence of MS authority for his alteration); and that the 1669 editor reverted to the original reading, not on the ground of disagreement with that interpretation, but because original authority favoured the reading 'they'. This explanation may be supported by the fact that the 1669 editor enclosed the words 'which . . . passe' in brackets, a feature which was retained in the 1719 edition. It is, however, hard to determine which meaning he was trying to indicate. Whatever the true explanation of the seventeenth-century textual changes, though, I prefer the interpretation that 'they' refers to 'times'. The sense of ll. 3–5 then is, I believe, that the sun, the time-maker itself, which paradoxically makes times in the very moment of their passing, is now older by a year, a measure of the time-sequence it had itself created.

4 *Is*] This applies grammatically only to the sun, but Donne is clearly making a similar assertion about everything mentioned in ll. 1 and 2.

6] all things except our love draw towards their destruction.

18 *inmates*] merely lodgers. Cf. Donne's letter to Sir Henry Goodyer (*c.* 1608): 'They [his vices] Inne not, but dwell in me'.
prove] experience.

19 *there above*] in heaven.

20] i.e. when death comes.

21 *throughly*] thoroughly.

22] 'But *in heaven* we shall be no more blessèd than anyone else.' (Grierson points out, however, that in fact the Scholastic Philosophy, to which Donne is probably alluding here, held that all are equally *content* in heaven, but *not* equally *blest*. Donne is therefore either inadvertently misinterpreting the Scholastic view, or wresting it in the interests of the poem.)

30 *threescore*] i.e. our diamond jubilee, as this is our anniversary.

A VALEDICTION: OF MY NAME, IN THE WINDOW

I

My name engrav'd herein
Doth cóntribute my firmness to this glass,
Which, ever since that charm, hath been
As hard as that which grav'd it was;
Thine eye will give it price enough to mock
The diamonds of either rock.

II

'Tis much that glass should be
As all-confessing, and through-shine as I;
'Tis more, that it shows thee to thee,
And clear reflects thee to thine eye.
But all such rules love's magic can undo,
Here you see me, and I am you.

III

As no one point, nor dash,
(Which are but áccessories to this name),
The showers and tempests can outwash,
So shall all times find me the same;
You this entireness better may fulfil,
Who have the pattern with you still.

IV

Or, if too hard and deep
This learning be, for a scratch'd name to teach,
It as a given death's head keep,
Lover's mortality to preach,
Or think this ragged bony name to be
My ruinous anatomy.

A VALEDICTION: OF MY NAME, IN THE WINDOW

Note on the title: 'Of' = 'on', as in the title of Hume's early philosophical work, *A Treatise of Human Nature.*

4 *that which grav'd it*] i.e. a diamond.

6 *diamonds*] trisyllabic.

6] As Chambers points out, this means diamonds either from the East or from the West Indies, from Golconda or from Brazil.

8 *through-shine*] 'transparent': cf. one of the verse Letters to the Countess of Bedford (Works, ed. Grierson, I. 218), l. 27.

9–10] The Luttrell MS (*Lut*) has an interesting reading:

'Tis more, that it shows thee to me,
And clear reflects me to thine eye.

This brings out the transparency of the window, whereas the normal reading suggests reflection in a mirror, and is, moreover, repetitive.

13 *point*] stop.

14] the parentheses, which fit well in a modern recension, are in fact the reading of the Luttrell MS.

14 *áccessories*] the only accentuation of the word in Donne's time.

17–18] I think the meaning of these somewhat obscure lines is: 'You may complete this utter devotion (i.e. by reciprocating it) better, by having the pattern (i.e. the durable letters of my name in the window) always with you.'

21 *as a given death's head*] like a present of a *memento mori* in a ring, as Chambers points out.

23 *ragged bony name*] Mr Henn has suggested to me that the name 'John Donne' would have presented a particularly ragged appearance. I think this would certainly have been so if it had been written in secretary hand. This may, however, be thinking too precisely on the line. Any name scratched on glass might easily appear ragged.

24] The sense of the line is probably that his skeleton is *dilapidated* through having lost the flesh, muscle, sinews, and veins, rather than that it has itself fallen into decay. It remains as the mere roof-tree and rafters of the house. The word 'dilapidated', the modern equivalent of 'ruinous', would, however, normally be applied to the house in such a case, not to the roof-tree and rafters.

25 *all my souls*] i.e. the vegetative, sensitive, and intellectual souls, of Scholastic philosophy.

28–30] Cf. possibly the resurrection of the dry bones, in *Ezekiel* (xxxvii. 1–10), as Mr Henn has suggested to me.

31–2] make my scattered body into a compact whole again, in this way, viz. by nursing my souls, whose action will clothe my skeleton again with muscle, sinew, vein, and so on.

33–42] 'Just as the strong powers with which the stars have been impregnated by the angels' (cf. Dante, *Paradiso*, ii. 127–9 and xxii. 112–23) 'are said to flow into the magic characters traced out when those stars are in the ascendant, so, since this name was cut when love and grief were in the ascendant, it will make you as much more loving as it

V

Then, as all my souls be
Emparadis'd in you (in whom alone
I understand, and grow, and see),
The rafters of my body, bone,
Being still with you, the muscle, sinew, and vein,
Which tile this house, will come again.

VI

Till my return, repair
And recompact my scattered body so.
As all the virtuous powers which are
Fix'd in the stars, are said to flow
Into such characters as gravèd be
When these stars have supremacy:

VII

So, since this name was cut
When love and grief their exaltation had,
No door 'gainst this name's influence shut;
As much more loving, as more sad,
'Twill make thee; and thou shouldst, till I return,
Since I die daily, daily mourn.

VIII

When thy inconsiderate hand
Flings out this casement, with my trembling name,
To look on one, whose wit or land
New battery to thy heart may frame,
Then think this name alive, and that thou thus
In it offend'st my Genius.

IX

And when thy melted maid,
Corrupted by thy lover's gold, and page,
His letter at thy pillow‿hath laid,
Disputed it, and tam'd thy rage,
And thou begin'st to thaw towards him, for this,
May my name step in, and hide his.

X

And if this treason go
To an overt act, and that thou write again,
In superscribing, this name flow
Into thy fancy, from the pane.
So, in forgetting, thou rememb'rest right,
And unaware to me shalt write.

XI

But glass and lines must be
No means our firm substantial love to keep;
Near death inflicts this lethargy,
And this I murmur in my sleep;
Impute this idle talk to that I go,
For dying men talk often so.

---

makes you sadder, and therefore do not shut out its influence. In any case, even your being sadder in itself will not be inappropriate as long as I am absent; for since I die every day (through being absent from you), you should mourn me every day.'

44 *out*] I have adopted this reading of the overwhelming number of MSS, against the more cautious 'ope' of the printed editions, retained by Grierson. My main internal reason is that the reading 'flings out' describes the action unambiguously, whereas the reading 'ope' does not.

46] may lay fresh siege to your heart.

48 *Genius*] protecting spirit.

49 *melted*] 'softened', i.e. into supporting the lover's cause.

50 *and*] a few MSS, including *Lut*, and the 1669 edition, read 'or', a more ironical reading, since it suggests that one of the two agents of corruption would suffice.

52 *Disputed it*] argued in favour of it.

55–6] An allusion to the legal distinction between treasonable intent, and treason manifested in an overt act.

57 *this name flow*] i.e. may this name flow (cf. l. 54).

61–4] 'But this is all absurd. We mustn't rely on glass and lines to preserve our firm, substantial love; it is the fact that I am nearly dead that has made me fall into this coma, and I'm murmuring all this in my sleep.' Cf. in a letter from Donne to Sir Henry Goodyer (*Letters*, ed. 1651, p. 57): 'and I may die yet, if talking idly be an ill sign.'

65 *go*] 'am going away' (which for him as a lover is tantamount to dying (cf. *The Legacy*, ll. 1–2)).

TWICKENHAM GARDEN

Blasted with sighs, and surrounded with tears,
  Hither I come to seek the spring,
  And at mine eyes, and at mine ears,
Receive such balms as else cure everything;
  But oh, self-traitor, I do bring
The spider love, which transubstantiates all,
  And can convert manna to gall;
And that this place may thoroughly be thought
  True Paradise, I have the serpent brought.

'Twere wholesomer for me, that winter did
  Benight the glory of this place,
  And that a grave frost did forbid
These trees to laugh, and mock me to my face;
  But that I may not this disgrace
Endure, nor leave this garden, Love, let me
  Some senseless piece of this place be;
Make me a mandrake, so I may groan here,
  Or a stone fountain weeping out my year.

Hither with crystal vials, lovers, come,
  And take my tears, which are love's wine,
  And try your mistress' tears at home,
For all are false, that taste not just like mine;
  Alas, hearts do not in eyes shine,
Nor can you more judge woman's thoughts by tears,
  Than by her shadow, what she wears.
O perverse sex, where none is true but she
  Who's therefore true, because her truth kills me.

Twickenham Park was the residence of Donne's friend, the Countess of Bedford, from 1608 to 1618.

1 *surrounded with tears*] 'overwhelmed by a flood of tears'. *Overflowed* is, as Grierson says, the root idea of 'surrounded' (late Lat. *superundare*), whose use in this sense became obsolete soon after Donne's time.

6–7] Alluding, as Chambers has pointed out, to the popular belief that spiders were full of poison.

6 *transubstantiates all*] 'changes everything into another substance'.

There is probably also an ironical allusion to the Roman Catholic doctrine of transubstantiation.

7 *manna to gall*] having both the sense of the conversion of something typically sweet to something typically bitter, *and* the sense of the conversion of nourishment of the soul into something bitterly working against spiritual health and poise.

9 *the serpent*] the great tempter, mentioned possibly because Donne knows that what he wants is sinful.

10 *'Twere wholesomer for me*] i.e. it would make me less miserable.
that] if.

12 *grave*] probably intended as a play on (1) heavy, (2) austere. This play is achieved in modern English by 'severe'.

15 *nor leave this garden*] I have ventured to revert here to the reading of the 1635–69 editions, and of the vast majority of the MSS. It seems to me to fit the sense of the stanza better than the reading of the 1633 edition 'nor yet leave loving' adopted by Chambers and Grierson. There is, however, much to be said for the latter reading. It is noteworthy that in several of the Group I MSS this half-line is omitted altogether (see Donne's Poetical Works, ed. Grierson, Oxford, 1912, vol. II, p. 26).

16 *senseless*] insensible.

17 *mandrake*] Mandrakes have forked roots, and were popularly supposed to groan when uprooted. (They do, in fact, make a grating noise when withdrawn from light soil.) Presumably, however, Donne wishes to be able to groan more than once, so he is probably referring to a mandrake as *something which groans*. The belief that the mandrake was an aphrodisiac and a promoter of conception appears to have persisted from very ancient times through classical antiquity and the Middle Ages (see J. R. Harris's article, *The Origin of the Cult of Aphrodite* in *Bulletin of the John Rylands Library*, October–December, 1916, where an attempt is made to prove that Aphrodite was originally only a personification of the mandrake). Donne *may* be suggesting that if he were a mandrake he might stimulate some love in the Countess. (For further information on the mandrake see the excellent note by Mr F. L. Lucas in his edition of Webster (vol. I. 227–8).)

17–18] If Donne were a mandrake or a stone fountain his groaning or weeping would be inconspicuous, for a mandrake *has* to groan, and a fountain *has* to weep. He would also himself be insensitive to the intolerable present situation.

18] Grierson, in his note in *Metaphysical Poetry: Donne to Butler*, quotes a parallel from Petrarch (Canz., xxiii. 115 f.).

21 *try*] test.

26 *true*] faithful.

26–7] This may mean 'O perverse sex, no member of which is faithful except the one who is quite certainly faithful, because her faithfulness (to another) kills me.' Alternatively, it may mean that she is herself perversely being faithful with the deliberate purpose of killing Donne.

A VALEDICTION: OF THE BOOK

I'll tell thee now, dear love, what thou shalt do
To anger destiny, as she doth us;
How I shall stay, though she eloign me thus,
And how posterity shall know it too;
How thine may out-endure
Sibyl's glory, and obscure
Her who from Pindar could allure,
And her, through whose help Lucan is not lame,
And her, whose book (they say) Homer did find, and name.

Study our manuscripts, those myriads
Of letters, which have past 'twixt thee and me,
Thence write our Annals, and in them will be,
To all whom love's subliming fire invades,
Rule and example found;
There, the faith of any ground
No schísmatic will dare to wound,
That sees, how Love this grace to us affords,
To make, to keep, to use, to be, these his Recórds,—

This book, as long-liv'd as the elements,
Or as the world's form, this all-gravèd tome
In cypher writ, or new-made idiom;
We for Love's clergy only are instruments,
When this book is made thus;
Should again the ravenous
Vandals and Goths inúndate us,
Learning were safe; in this our Universe
Schools might learn sciences, spheres music, angels verse.

Here Love's divines (since all divinity
Is love or wonder) may find all they seek,
Whether abstract spiritual love they like,
Their souls exhal'd with what they do not see,

A VALEDICTION: OF THE BOOK

3 *eloign*] 'takes me away' (Old French: *esloignier*, Fr. *éloigner:* 1633 edition spells 'Esloygne').

6 *Sibyl's glory*] the fame of the Cumaean Sibyl.

7] Corinna the Theban (fl. B.C. 500), who instructed Pindar in poetry, and subsequently defeated him five times at Thebes. (See Aelian, *Variae Historiae*, xiii. 25.)

8] Lucan's wife, Polla Argentaria, was reputed to have 'assisted her husband in correcting the first three Books of his *Pharsalia*'.

9] The tradition which fits this line best is that referred to by Lemprière, that Homer obtained from a sacred scribe at Memphis a work on the siege of Troy, by a certain Phantasia of Memphis. Professor Norton raises the alternative possibility, which appears to me less probable, that the line refers to Helena, the daughter of the pseudo-Musaeus. (See the *Myriobiblion* of Photius.)

13 *subliming fire*] 'purifying fire'; the chemical process of sublimation consists in converting a solid into vapour by heat, and then re-converting it into a solid by cooling; the sublimate is purer than the original solid.

15–16] No schismatic will dare to attack the truth of any fundamental doctrine expressed there.

17 *That sees*] i.e. if he sees.

18] I feel unable to agree with Grierson's emendation of the comma to a full stop at the end of this line, and I have restored the comma of the 1633–69 editions. The passage seems to me to make perfect sense with the old punctuation (see note on ll. 21–2, below). I have, however, added a dash, to make clear to the modern reader the continuity of sense between this stanza and the next.

20 *tome*] This is the reading of the 1633 and 1635 editions, adopted by Grierson; and I have little doubt that it is correct. Some MSS, including the good MSS *C57* and *Lec*, read 'Tomb' or 'tombe', and this was the reading adopted in the 1669 edition. Although I do not believe that reading to be right, I do think there is a play here on 'tome' and 'tomb' in 'all-graved tome'. (Cf. *The Autumnal*: 'He doth not dig a *Grave*, but build a *Tombe*'.)

21–2] Through his understanding of the first three lines of the stanza as an absolute clause, Grierson naturally emended the semi-colon after 'idiom' to a comma, and the comma after 'instruments' to a colon. The first three lines of the stanza, however, seem to me to make excellent sense as a clause in apposition to the word 'Records' at the end of the preceding stanza; and I have therefore ventured to restore the punctuation of the editions of 1633–69.

22–3] I think the more probable interpretation of these lines is: 'We shall be documents exclusively for Love's clergy when this book has been made in the way just described.' I do not agree with Grierson's interpretation at this point. He takes 'only' to refer to instruments. This interpretation seems to me to have no advantage; whereas the

Or, loth so to amuse
Faith's infirmity, they choose
Something which they may see and use;
For, though mind be the heaven, where love doth sit,
Beauty a convenient type may be to figure it.

Here, more than in their books, may lawyers find
Both by what titles mistresses are ours,
And how prerogative these states devours,
Transferr'd from Love himself, to womankind;
Who, though from heart, and eyes,
They exact great subsidies,
Forsake him who on them relies,
And for the cause, honour, or conscience, give—
Chimeras, vain as they, or their prerogative.

Here statesmen (or of them, they which can read)
May of their occupation find the grounds:
Love and their art alike it deadly wounds,
If to consider what 'tis, one proceed;
In both they do excel
Who the present govern well,
Whose weakness none doth, or dares, tell;
In this thy book, such will their nothing see,
As in the Bible some can find out alchemy.

Thus vent thy thoughts; abroad I'll study thee,
As he removes far off, that great heights takes;
How great love is, presence best trial makes,
But absence tries how long this love will be;
To take a latitude,
Sun, or stars, are fitliest view'd
At their brightest, but to conclude
Of longitudes, what other way have we,
But to mark when, and where, the dark eclipses be?

interpretation which I have suggested brings out the point that *only* 'Love's clergy' will be able to read the book. This accords with Donne's doctrine of the exclusiveness of the sect of true lovers, and with his view of love as a mystery, which has its adepts. Cf. for instance

'Twere profanation of our joys
 To tell the laity our love.
(*A Valediction: forbidding mourning*)

It also fits in well with ll. 24–7. Since the book will be written in cypher or in a new-made idiom understood by no one but 'Love's clergy', the invaders would not understand the book, and it would therefore be preserved as innocuous, and survive as a compendium of all arts and sciences, so that culture would be saved.

25 *inundate*] I wholeheartedly follow Grierson's adoption of the reading of almost all the MSS, as against 'invade', the reading of the printed editions. Grierson gives ample support in Donne's own usage, e.g. in *Essays in Divinity*: 'The inundation of the Goths in Italy.' Grierson has also mentioned to me such a use in Bacon's *Advancement of Learning*: and I have myself found one in the *Novum Organum*.

26 *Universe*] Mr Ingram has drawn my attention to one of the definitions of 'universe' in Webster's Dictionary (1920 edn), viz. 'Any distinct field or province of thought or reality conceived as forming a closed system or self-inclusive and independent organization.' This may well be the sense here, implying the self-sufficiency and comprehensiveness of their love.

31 *exhal'd with*] drawn out by.

32 *amuse*] tantalize.

36 *figure*] symbolize.

37–45] 'Here (in this book made of our letters) lawyers may find, better than in their legal treatises, the nature of our titles to our mistresses, and also how these estates of ours (in our mistresses) are eaten up by the prerogative (to exact feudal dues over and above those which were customary) which belongs of right to the lord, Love, but has been transferred to womankind. Women, although they claim large payments from the hearts and eyes of men, do not perform their part of the feudal bargain, but forsake the men who rely on them, and give as excuse for doing so, "honour" or "conscience", which are mere figments of the imagination, as empty as they themselves and their prerogative are.'

37] To bring out the sense I have added commas after 'Here' and 'books', and removed a comma after 'find'.

46–54] 'Here statesmen (or rather, those statesmen who can read) will be able to discover the principles of their profession. Both love and politics are unable to stand scrutiny without collapsing under it. In both spheres of activity the most successful practitioners are the opportunists, who either take other people in, or make them afraid to expose them. In this book of yours, such people will see the emptiness of their art, just as some people learn alchemy from the Bible' (*or* 'discover alchemy in the Bible'). (The sense being: 'Your book deals with genuine deep love, but will nevertheless teach what sham love is, just as the Bible can teach the humbug science of alchemy.')

55 *vent*] i.e. write down.
abroad I'll study thee] 'While I'm abroad I'll read the Annals (cf. l. 12) you have written.'

56 *removes far off*] moves away to a good distance. *takes*] surveys.

57–8] Presence is the best test how big love is: but absence tests its endurance.

59–61] As Grierson points out, 'the latitude of any spot may always be found by measuring the distance from the zenith, of a star whose altitude, i.e. distance from the equator, is known.' There seems to me, however, almost certainly a further point here in 'at their brightest' beyond merely the contrast with 'dark eclipses', mentioned by Grierson: namely, that it was at least a common belief that stars were brightest when highest in the sky, i.e. nearest the zenith, and therefore when their distance from the zenith was easiest to measure.

59–63] The comparison is a highly fanciful one, almost resting on a purely verbal basis. Grierson thought it did so entirely. It seems to me, however, that there is, first, a slight secondary suggestion of size or bulk in the word 'latitude'. There may also *perhaps* be a more substantial justification for one leg of the comparison, namely that latitude corresponds to intensity of light or heat.

61–3] I cannot do better than reproduce a part of Grierson's note: 'If the time at which an instantaneous phenomenon, such as an eclipse of the moon, begins at Greenwich (or whatever be the first meridian) is known, and the time of its beginning at whatever place a ship is, be then noted, the difference gives the longitude. The eclipses of the moons of Saturn have been used for the purpose. The method is not, however, a practically useful one.'

COMMUNITY

General Note: There is a passage strikingly related to the guiding thought of this poem in one of Donne's *Paradoxes* (IV): 'And of *Indifferent* things many things are become perfectly good by being *Common*, as *Customs* by use are made binding *Lawes*. But I remember nothing that is therefore *ill*, because it is *Common*, but *Women, of whom also: they that are most Common, are the best of that Occupation they profess.*'

2 *still*] Most probably Donne is simply using 'still' as meaning 'always', a common use at that time; the sense therefore being 'For evil is always evil, and good is always good.'

5 *prove*] try.

12] this is the only possibility left, that all men may use all women.

17 *waste*] in the old spelling 'wast', the rhyme being perfect.

18 *nor . . . nor*] neither . . . nor.

21 *doth as well*] do equally well.

COMMUNITY

Good we must love, and must hate ill,
For ill is ill, and good good, still,
But there are things indifferent,
Which we may neither hate, nor love,
But one, and then another prove,
As we shall find our fancy bent.

If then at first wise Nature had
Made women either good or bad,
Then some we might hate, and some choose:
But since she did them so create,
That we may neither love, nor hate,
Only this rests: All, all may use.

If they were good it would be seen,
Good is as visible as green,
And to all eyes itself betrays:
If they were bad, they could not last,
Bad doth itself, and others, waste;
So, they deserve nor blame, nor praise.

But they are ours as fruits are ours,
He that but tastes, he that devours,
And he that leaves all, doth as well:
Chang'd loves are but chang'd sorts of meat;
And when he hath the kernel eat,
Who doth not fling away the shell?

LOVE'S GROWTH
or
SPRING

I scarce believe my love to be so pure
  As I had thought it was,
  Because it doth endure
Vicissitude, and season, as the grass;
Methinks I lied all winter, when I swore
My love was infinite, if spring make it more.
But if this medicine, love, which cures all sorrow
With more, not only be no quíntessence,
But mix'd of all stuffs paining soul, or sense,
And of the Sun his working vigour borrow,
Love's not so pure, and abstract, as they use
To say, which have no mistress but their muse,
But as all else, being elemented too,
Love sometimes would contémplate, sometimes do.

And yet no greater, but more eminent,
  Love by the spring is grown;
  As, in the firmament,
Stars by the Sun are not enlarg'd, but shown.
Gentle love deeds, as blossoms on a bough,
From love's awakened root do bud out now.
If, as in water stirr'd more circles be
Produc'd by one, love such additions take,
Those, like so many spheres, but one heaven make,
For they are all concentric unto thee:
And though each spring do add to love new heat,
As princes do in times of action get
New taxes, and remit them not in peace,
No winter shall abate the spring's increase.

Note on the title: Love's Growth was the title given in the printed editions, and some MSS. Other MSS, including some of high authority, give *Spring*.

Note on the layout: The 1633 edition and some MSS break the poem after l. 6. Other MSS do not: and as the asymmetricality is untypical of the *Songs and Sonets*, I have closed up stanza 1.

LOVE'S GROWTH or SPRING

Further Note on the layout: Grierson, in his plain text (Oxford, 1929), removes the asymmetricality by adopting the break after line 6 and introducing a corresponding break after line 20. This alternative is supported by Mr John Sparrow in a letter to *TLS*, 21 Dec. 1956. He rightly urges that only one other of the *Songs and Sonets* has stanzas as long as fourteen lines. After careful consideration, however, I have decided to retain the layout I had adopted. My reasons are three: (1) That there is no other of the *Songs and Sonets* in stanzas of different lengths; (2) that none of the MSS or old editions give a break after line 20, whereas in some MSS the layout is that here presented; (3) that such a break would not correspond to a break in sense.

8 *quintessence*] Grierson quotes a key passage from Paracelsus (*The Fourth Book of the Archidoxies. Concerning the Quintessence*) which refers to the quintessence as being a certain matter which could be extracted from all natural bodies, and which was absolutely pure, and separate from the four elements. It had the capacity to cure all diseases, and did not do this by means of temperature, but by its own purity. It was not to be extracted 'by the mixture or addition of incongruous matters'. Elsewhere Paracelsus says that it is not a fifth element.

9] 'but a mixture of every substance which is painful to the soul or the senses.' In the belief that this is the correct meaning, I have removed the comma after 'stuffs', so as to exclude useless ambiguity.

10] 'owes its strength to the sun' (and is therefore stronger in the spring than it was in the winter).

13] But being, like everything else, composed of diverse elements.

15 *eminent*] conspicuous.

17–18] A difficult passage. I think that Grierson's excellent note is probably right in interpreting the lines to mean: 'The stars at sunrise are not really made larger, but they are made to seem larger' (op. cit., II. 31). The working of the simile may perhaps be made clearer by quoting a similar though not precisely parallel passage from Dryden's *Heroic Stanzas on the Death of Oliver Cromwell* (stanza 6):

His grandeur he derived from heaven alone;
For he was great ere fortune made him so;
And wars, like mists that rise against the sun,
Made him but greater seem, not greater grow.

21–4] 'If love acquires additions of that sort' (i.e. 'gentle love deeds'), 'just as when water is stirred additional circles are produced by the original one, then these new additions will only constitute one heaven, just as the spheres in the Ptolemaic astronomy only form one heaven; and that is because all these additions will be centred on you, just as in that system the spheres are all centred on the earth.'

26–7] *in times of action get New taxes*] levy new taxes in times of emergency.

LOVE'S EXCHANGE

Love, any devil else but you
Would for a given soul give something too.
At Court your fellows every day
Give the art of rhyming, huntsmanship, or play,
For them which were their own before;
Only I have nothing which gave more,
But am, alas, by being lowly, lower.

I ask no dispensation now
To falsify a tear, or sigh, or vow,
I do not sue from thee to draw
A *non obstante* on nature's law;
These are prerogatives, they inhere
In thee and thine; none should forswear
Except that he Love's minion were.

Give me thy weakness, make me blind,
Both ways, as thou and thine, in eyes and mind;
Love, let me never know that this
Is love, or, that love childish is;
Let me not know that others know
That she knows my pains, lest that so
A tender shame make me mine own new woe.

If thou give nothing, yet thou art just,
Because I would not thy first motions trust;
Small towns, which stand stiff, till great shot
Enforce them, by war's law condition not.
Such in love's warfare is my case;
I may not article for grace,
Having put Love at last to show this face:

LOVE'S EXCHANGE

3–5] At Court your colleagues (i.e. the devils who preside over rhyming, hunting, and gambling) bestow every day the art of rhyming, huntsmanship, or gambling, on those who are already their devotees.

6] I alone have received nothing, although I gave more of myself than those devotees of the devils of rhyming, hunting, and gambling did.

8–14] A stanza of some difficulty. I do not think its true sense is usually understood. I believe the meaning to be as follows: 'I am not asking now for any dispensation to counterfeit a tear, sigh or vow; I am not asking you for an exemption from the law of nature. Such counterfeiting is an exclusive privilege belonging by nature to you and your train of followers; nobody should perjure himself unless he is one of Love's dependants.' The key to a true understanding of this stanza seems to me to be the word 'now' in l. 8. It is easy to misunderstand the stanza if this word is not given its full force. The point is that *now* that he is one of Love's dependants, the poet does not need dispensations and exemptions in order to commit perjury, since it is the natural thing for lovers to do this. It will be seen from my suggested interpretation that I do not agree with Grierson's view that 'minion' (l. 14) is used here in the sense of 'one specially favoured or beloved'. I think it is used as meaning simply a 'dependant'.

23 *motions*] probably a play on two of the senses in use at that time: (1) 'proposals', (2) 'impulses communicated'.

24–5] 'It is one of the laws of war that small towns which hold out against a siege until reduced by heavy artillery, may not attach conditions to their surrender.'

27–8] 'I cannot stipulate for mercy, when I have caused Love in the end to adopt this attitude towards me' (with a play on 'show this woman's face to me', the sense which is taken up fully in the next stanza).

28] As Mr F. L. Lucas has suggested to me, the continuation of the sense in the next stanza seems to require a lighter stop than the full stop printed by the early editions and all modern editors. I have therefore ventured to print a colon, which has the added advantage of emphasizing the anaphora.

This face, by which he could command
And change the idolatry of any land;
This face, which, whereso'er it comes,
Can call vow'd men from cloisters, dead from tombs,
And melt both poles at once, and store
Deserts with cities, and make more
Mines in the earth, than quarries were before.

For this, Love is enrag'd with me,
Yet kills not. If I must example be
To future rebels; if the unborn
Must learn, by my being cut up, and torn:
Kill, and dissect me, Love; for this
Torture against thine own end is,—
Rack'd carcasses make ill anatomies.

29 *This face*] i.e. his mistress's face.

30] and make any country adopt a new and true worship (i.e. of this woman, or of Love). There may possibly be a jibe here (and in l. 32) against Roman Catholicism.

31–5] The vitalizing force of the woman is what is here particularized in the sequence of references: to renunciation of celibacy, re-animation of dead bodies, thawing of the frozen poles into fertility, filling of deserts with the teeming life of cities, and increase of the earth's rich active mineral deposits. It is not inconceivable that Donne may have intended to contrast the animating and constructive power of this 'face' with the destructiveness of the 'face' of Marlowe's Helen. I owe this last suggestion to Mr Ingram.

34–5] There may be reference here to the belief current in Donne's time that the heat of the sun's rays transmuted baser into more precious metals.

36 *For this*] i.e. for holding out against him for so long.

41 *against thine own end is*] militates against your own purpose.

42] 'Bodies which have been tortured do not make good subjects for dissection.'

CONFINED LOVE

Some man unworthy to be possessor
Of old or new love, himself being false or weak,
Thought his pain and shame would be lesser,
If on womankind he might his anger wreak;
And thence a law did grow,
One might but one man know;
But are other creatures so?

Are sun, moon, or stars by law forbidden
To smile where they list, or lend away their light?
Are birds divorc'd, or are they chidden
If they leave their mate, or lie abroad a-night?
Beasts do not jointures lose
Though they new lovers choose,
But we are made worse than those.

Who e'er rigg'd fair ship to lie in harbours,
And not to seek new lands, or not to deal withal?
Or built fair houses, set trees, and arbors,
Only to lock up, or else to let them fall?
Good is not good, unless
A thousand it possess,
But doth waste with greediness.

CONFINED LOVE

11 *a-night*] The reading of the 1633–54 editions and of those MSS I have seen is 'a night'; but I think Grierson and Hayward right in taking this to mean 'at night' rather than 'for a night, from time to time'. Their interpretation seems to fit better with l. 20, and indeed with the first half of l. 11 itself.

16 *deal withal*] trade with it.

20 *it possess*] possess it.

THE DREAM

Dear love, for nothing less than thee
Would I have broke this happy dream;
It was a theme
For reason, much too strong for phantasy,
Therefore thou wak'dst me wisely; yet
My dream thou brok'st not, but continuedst it,
Thou art so truth, that thoughts of thee suffice
To make dreams truths, and fables histories;
Enter these arms, for since thou thought'st it best
Not to dream all my dream, let's act the rest.

As lightning, or a taper's light,
Thine eyes, and not thy noise, wak'd me;
Yet I thought thee
(Thou lovest truth) but an Angel, at first sight,
But when I saw thou sawest my heart,
And knew'st my thoughts, beyond an Angel's art,
When thou knew'st what I dreamt, when thou knew'st when
Excess of joy would wake me, and cam'st then,
I must confess, it could not choose but be
Profaneness, to think thee anything but thee.

Coming and staying show'd thee, thee,
But rising makes me doubt, that now
Thou art not thou.
That love is weak, where fear's as strong as he;
'Tis not all spirit, pure, and brave,
If mixture it of *fear*, *shame*, *honour*, have.
Perchance, as torches which must ready be
Men light and put out, so thou deal'st with me,
Thou cam'st to kindle, goest to come; thus I
Will dream that hope again, but else would die.

THE DREAM

There are striking similarities of idea and expression between this poem and Donne's *Elegy X* (*The Dreame*).

3–4] 'It was a suitable subject for a fully wakened consciousness and much too convincing to form part of a mere dream.'

7] *Thou art so truth*] 'You are so essentially Truth.' Grierson aptly quotes a passage from Aquinas, in which it is asserted of God that truth is not merely *in* Him, but He is himself the highest and first Truth. As Grierson points out, Donne is therefore crediting his lady with one of the divine attributes.

10 *Not to dream all my dream*] i.e. for me not to dream all my dream.
act] many MSS read 'do'. That reading is physically stronger. It is not out of the question that Donne toned it down. *TCC* reads 'act'.

14 (*Thou lovest truth*)] The reading of many MSS. I think the sense of the words is: 'If you really want to know the truth, as I expect you do.'
but an Angel] 'merely an Angel'. I have decided to adopt this reading of a number of the MSS, including some of very high authority, in preference to the reading of the 1633–69 editions, which omit the word 'but'. The insertion of the word seems to me a bold and surprising touch characteristic of Donne: and the phrase fits well with the sense of l. 16 (see below). I should not be surprised if the 1633 editor had taken the step of omitting 'but'. It would have been natural enough for an editor already troubled with censorship. The present case is different from that of l. 10; for even *TCC* reads 'but'.

16] Grierson's note has thrown much light on this line. As he points out, the sense is not that she could read his thoughts better than an angel, but that she could read his thoughts whereas an angel could not: the reading of thoughts being beyond the power of angels, according to the view of Aquinas, which Donne preferred to the opposite view of the Scotists (see *LXXX Sermons*, XI. 111, quoted Grierson).

19–20 *it . . . Profaneness*] 'it would necessarily be profanity.'

20 *Profaneness*] I have ventured to adopt this reading of all the MSS cited by Grierson, and of such other MSS as I have seen, in preference to the reading of the printed editions 'profane'. The curtailment seems to me just the sort of alteration an editor not responsive to the finer points of Donne's rhythms might have made, in order to achieve a line apparently more regular, though actually much weaker.

21 *show'd thee, thee*] showed you to be yourself.

22 *doubt*] suspect.

27–9] 'Perhaps, in the same way as when torches have to be dry enough to light at once when required, people light them beforehand, and then put them out, so you came to set me alight, and are now only going away for a short while before you return to light me again.'

29 *thus*] This is the reading of the majority and the most reliable of the MSS: and I have ventured to adopt it in preference to 'then', the reading of the printed editions followed by Grierson. It seems to me to have somewhat more finality.

A VALEDICTION: OF WEEPING

Let me pour forth
My tears before thy face, whilst I stay here,
For thy face coins them, and thy stamp they bear,
And by this mintage they are something worth,
For thus they be
Pregnant of thee;
Fruits of much grief they are, emblems of more,
When a tear falls, that thou falls which it bore,
So thou and I are nothing then, when on a diverse shore.

On a round ball
A workman that hath copies by, can lay
An Europe, Afric, and an Asia,
And quickly make that, which was nothing, *All*;
So doth each tear
Which thee doth wear,
A globe, yea world, by that impression grow,
Till thy tears mixt with mine do overflow
This world, by waters sent from thee, my heaven dissolvèd so.

O more than Moon,
Draw not up seas to drown me in thy sphere,
Weep me not dead, in thine arms, but forbear
To teach the sea, what it may do too soon;
Let not the wind
Example find
To do me more harm than it purposeth;
Since thou and I sigh one another's breath,
Whoe'er sighs most, is cruellest, and hastes the other's death.

A VALEDICTION: OF WEEPING

Note on the title: 'Of' = 'on'.

2 *whilst I stay here*] while I am still with you.

3] It is possible, though not certain, that this line refers to two processes: (1) the causing of the poet's tears by the sight of his lady's face (coining); and (2) the reflection of her face in his tears (stamping).

6 *Pregnant*] full.

7–9] A difficult passage. The reading of the MSS for l. 8 is as given. The 1633 edition reads:

When a teare falls, that thou falst which it bore,

and that is the reading adopted by Grierson in all his editions. I have discussed the passage with him, and he has told me that he now considers the MS reading superior. I understand from him that that is also the view of Miss Helen Gardner, of St Hilda's College, Oxford, the editor of the *Divine Poems*. The MS reading has already been adopted by Mr John Hayward in the Nonesuch Donne, and I entirely agree with him that the reading of the 1633 edition was the sort of error one would expect of a short-sighted printer. The word 'that' was evidently understood by the 1633 editor (who may well have been the printer himself), as a conjunction, whereas it is in fact a demonstrative adjective. The sense of that line, then, is: 'When one of my tears falls, that particular Thou falls which the tear carried in it' (i.e. 'the image of you in the tear falls').

The sense of the whole passage then appears to me to be as follows: 'My tears are the result of much grief (at the thought of parting from you), and they are emblems of more grief to come (the grief of being absent from you); when one of my tears falls, that particular Thou which the tear carried in it also falls, and both my tear and your image perish; and this is emblematic of what will happen when we are parted; you, like your image in the tear, will be nothing then, and I, like my tear, will be nothing too.' Donne is continually referring to the absence of lovers as a sort of death.

9 *when on a diverse shore*] 'when we are in different countries with the sea between us'.

10 *round ball*] globe.

10–13] Difficulty is often experienced in seizing the exact image here. I think it is almost certainly that of an artificer *pasting* a map on a globe. He will need more than one piece of mapped paper ('copy') to cover a sphere, and that may account for the plural 'copies'. There is an interesting passage in a letter from Donne to Sir Robert Carre (1624) in which the procedure is referred to: 'And you know, that though the labour of any ordinary Artificer in that Trade will bring East and West together, (for if a flat Map be pasted upon a round Globe, the farthest East, and the farthest West meet, and are all one) yet all this brings not North and South a scruple of a degree the nearer.'

14–15 *each tear Which thee doth wear*] This phrase is the subject of controversy. The point at issue is whether the word 'tear' refers to a tear of Donne's or to a tear of his beloved's. I personally think it refers to a tear of Donne's. There is certainly no definite mention of her tears until l. 17, and hitherto in the poem his tears have been 'wearing' her image.

15] which bears your impression.

16 *A globe, yea world*] I think the sense is perhaps: 'a globe, no, more than that, a real world'.

17–18] Another crux. The focus of difficulty is the term 'this world', in l. 18. Does it mean (1) the real world, or (2) Donne himself, or (3) a tear of Donne's, or (4) a tear of his beloved's? If (1) is the right interpretation, then the general sense would seem to be: 'It is all very wonderful your creating worlds by merely appearing in my tear: but you spoil everything if you weep yourself. Our combined tears will bring another Flood upon the world, and its proportions as a flood will be caused by your weeping, and, furthermore, you will destroy yourself by doing it, which will be the end of my happiness, since you are my heaven.' Thus there will have been the Creation, the Flood, and, worse than all, the destruction of Heaven. If (2) is the right interpretation, the general sense would probably be: 'It is all very wonderful your creating worlds by merely appearing in my tear: but you will destroy me if you weep, and you will destroy yourself as well.' (2) has the advantage that it leads very naturally on to the sense of the next stanza. If (3) is the right interpretation, the general sense would seem to be: 'Each tear of mine by bearing your image grows into a world, but when you drench yourself with your own tears, that is like the flooding of the land on the world of my tear by waters coming from you, who are my heaven, and destroy yourself (and my happiness) by sending them.' Interpretation (4) would, in my view, result in nonsense. Between the other three interpretations I cannot, at present, make a definite choice: but I feel that (3) is *too* hyperingenious and fanciful, though it links well with l. 16. I do, in any case, feel convinced that the term 'this world' cannot mean *both* a tear and this world. Multiple meanings are not always wonderful.

18 *my heaven*] possibly alluding to the crystalline or watery heaven in the Ptolemaic astonomy. It is, I think, worth mentioning that the Luttrell MS places 'my heaven' in parentheses. This interesting reading would alter the sense, making 'dissolvèd' qualify 'this world', instead of 'my heaven'. This has the great attraction of connecting the sense of the two stanzas: and I have been sorely tempted to adopt the reading.

19–21] The sense of these lines I take to be: 'You, who are more powerful (and brighter, and more glamorous, and so on) than the moon, I beg and beseech you, do not attract seas to drown me, right up into your sphere' (the Moon's Sphere (First Sphere) or the Crystalline (Ninth) Sphere of the Ptolemaic system) 'where I now am; do not kill me by weeping, while I am in your very arms.' Mr Ingram has suggested to me that there may be an allusion to the Endymion story.

21 *in thine arms*] A wonderful touch. Here there seems to be real and useful multiplicity of meaning. The implication of 'in thine arms' seems to be threefold: (1) the last place in which I should feel dead; (2) the place where I am safe from the dangers of the world; (3) the place where you have me, not where you have lost me.

MUMMY
or
LOVE'S ALCHEMY

Some that have deeper digg'd love's mine than I,
Say, where his centric happiness doth lie:
    I have lov'd, and got, and told,
But should I love, get, tell, till I were old,
I should not find that hidden mystery;
    Oh, 'tis imposture all:
And as no chymic yet the Elixir got
    But glorifies his pregnant pot,
    If by the way to him befall
Some odoriferous thing, or med'cinal,
  So, lovers dream a rich and long delight,
  But get a winter-seeming summer's night.

Our ease, our thrift, our honour, and our day,
Shall we for this vain bubble's shadow pay?
    Ends love in this, that my man
Can be as happy as I can, if he can
Endure the short scorn of a bridegroom's play?
    That loving wretch that swears
'Tis not the bodies marry, but the minds,
    Which he in her angelic finds,
    Would swear as justly, that he hears,
In that day's rude hoarse minstrelsy, the spheres.
  Hope not for mind in women; at their best
  Sweetness and wit, they are but Mummy, possess'd.

MUMMY or LOVE'S ALCHEMY

Note on the title: I have supplied both the title given in most of the MSS, viz. *Mummy*, and the title *Love's Alchemy*, given in the 1633–69 editions, as it seems to me illuminating to have both at the head of the poem.

1–2] The direct reference of these lines is to the ethereal claims of high-minded lovers. Donne's scepticism as to the validity of such claims may, however, be latent here in the coarse secondary implications of some of the language. 'Centric', for instance, is used in Elegy XVIII with an obviously sexual sense:

> Although we see Celestial bodies move
> Above the earth, the earth we Till and Love:
> So we her ayres contemplate words and heart,
> And virtues; but we love the Centrique part. (ll. 33–6).

'Digg'd' in l. 1 of the present poem is also clearly paralleled by 'till' in the above passage.

2 *his centric happiness*] i.e. the core of love's happiness.

3 *told*] 'counted' (the 'successful' love affairs) or, possibly, 'calculated' (the essence of love) like an alchemist.

6] i.e. love has no 'centric happiness' as the 'deeper' lovers had boasted it had.

7 *chymic*] alchemist.
the Elixir] 'the *Elixir Vitae*, which heals all disease, and indefinitely prolongs life' (Grierson).

9] if during his quest he chance to hit on.

12] i.e. a short and cold time of it.

17] Endure the short humiliation of a wedding ceremony.

20] i.e. and that it is her mind which he finds angelic in his beloved.

22 *In that day's rude hoarse minstrelsy*] i.e. in the crude and raucous scrapings and blowings at the wedding day celebrations.
the spheres] i.e. the music of the spheres.

24 *Mummy*] 'body without mind'; but, more than that, 'mere lumps of dead flesh'. The belief that Egyptian mummies had been prepared with bitumen or asphalt had led medieval physicians in the East to prescribe first the scrapings off mummies, and then the mummified flesh itself, both for external and internal use. The term 'mummy' in time came to be applied to this dead flesh. A considerable trade in such 'mummy' was carried on between the Near East and Western Europe throughout the Middle Ages, and indeed, despite denunciation by eminent physicians like Paré, until the eighteenth, and in parts of Europe, the nineteenth century. Often enough the 'mummy' came to be a spurious manufacture from dead bodies of recent date, especially those of felons and suicides, doctored with bitumen and aloes, and baked until the embalming matter penetrated.

24] This is the punctuation Grierson derived from some of the MSS. The punctuation of the 1633–54 editions, which also makes sense, is

> at their best,
> Sweetnesse, and wit they are, but, Mummy, possest.

THE FLEA

Mark but this flea, and mark in this
How little that which thou deny'st me is;
Me it suck'd first, and now sucks thee,
And in this flea our two bloods mingled be;
Confess it: this cannot be said
A sin, or shame, or loss of maidenhead,
   Yet this enjoys before it woo,
   And pamper'd swells with one blood made of two,
   And this, alas, is more than we would do.

Oh stay, three lives in one flea spare,
Where we almost, nay more than married are:
This flea is you and I, and this
Our marriage bed, and marriage temple is;
Though parents grudge, and you, we're met
And cloister'd in these living walls of jet.
   Though use make you apt to kill me,
   Let not to that, self-murder added be,
   And sacrilege, three sins in killing three.

Cruel and sudden, hast thou since
Purpled thy nail in blood of innocence?
In what could this flea guilty be,
Except in that drop which it suck'd from thee?
Yet thou triumph'st, and say'st that thou
Find'st not thyself, nor me, the weaker now:
   'Tis true; then learn how false, fears be;
   Just so much honour, when thou yield'st to me,
   Will waste, as this flea's death took life from thee.

THE FLEA

Note on the text: It is clear that this poem underwent revision. The unrevised version seems to me clearly to have been that represented by the so-called Group I MSS (*D*, *H49*, *Lec*, *C57*, *SP*). This was the version printed in the 1633 edition and subsequent editions up to and including the 1654 edition. That version was adopted by Grierson.

The revised version seems to me that represented by the Group II MSS, including *TCC* and *TCD*. This version (with slight variations) was first printed in 1669. It seems to me to give a more finished and equally vital poem; and I have therefore reproduced here what seems to me the best text of that version.

5 *said*] called.

9 *alas*] i.e. because she will not yield to him.

11 *more than married*] possibly because their bloods are mingled in the flea: possibly because the flea is also their marriage-bed and marriage-temple: possibly for both reasons.

16] probably: 'though you are used to killing me with your coldness.'

18 *sacrilege*] because she will be attacking a temple (cf. l. 13).
three sins in killing three] murder in killing him, suicide in killing herself, and sacrilege in killing the flea.

THE CURSE

Whoever guesses, thinks, or dreams he knows
Who is my mistress, wither by this curse;
　　His only, and only his purse
　　May some dull heart to love dispose,
And she yield then to all that are his foes;
　May he be scorn'd by one, whom all else scorn,
　Forswear to others, what to her he hath sworn,
　With fear of missing, shame of getting, torn:

Madness his sorrow, gout his cramp, may he
Make, by but thinking who hath made him such:
　　And may he feel no touch
　　Of conscience, but of fame, and be
Anguish'd, not that 'twas sin, but that 'twas she:
　In early and long scarceness may he rot,
　For land which had been his, if he had not
　Himself incestuously an heir begot:

May he dream treason, and believe that he
Meant to perform it, and confess, and die,
　　And no recórd tell why:
　　His sons, which none of his may be,
Inherit nothing but his infamy:
　Or may he so long parasites have fed,
　That he would fain be theirs, whom he hath bred,
　And at the last be circumcis'd for bread:

The venom of all stepdames, gamesters' gall,
What tyrants, and their subjects, interwish,
　　What plants, mines, beasts, fowl, fish
　　Can cóntribute, all ill which all
Prophets, or poets, spake; And all which shall
　Be annex'd in schedules unto this by me,
　Fall on that man; for if it be a she,
　Nature beforehand hath out-cursèd me.

THE CURSE

3] Grierson seems to me clearly right in restoring the reading of the 1633–54 editions and of the MSS in place of 'Him, only for his purse . . .', the reading of the 1669 edition, followed by Chambers: but I do not feel happy about his explanation of the sense, namely: 'What is to dispose "some dull heart to love" is his *only* purse and *his* alone, no one's but his purse.' This is a *possible* interpretation; and, if it be accepted, a modern text should, I think, insert a comma after 'only his', to make the sense clearer. In my view, however, a more probable interpretation is: 'May the only purse he possesses, and nothing but that purse, attract some bore of a woman to love him.' ('His only purse', so that he may have nothing left when the woman has finished with him: 'only his purse', so that the woman will not care a rap for him when his money is gone.) Grierson tells me that he agrees.

While concurring in my account of l. 3, Mr F. L. Lucas has, however, indicated another difficulty, viz. that the word order does not accord with this interpretation since, e.g., 'Heaven may strike him!' is not good English for 'May heaven strike him!'. A possible answer might be that the word 'that' may be understood at the beginning of l. 3. Mr Lucas's objection has, however, suggested to me another possibility, namely, that the subject of 'dispose' is 'some dull heart', and that the verb is being used as a neuter verb in the obsolete sense (current in Donne's time), of 'to bargain', 'to agree on terms'. In that case ll. 3–4 could mean: 'May some bore of a woman agree to love the only purse he possesses, and only that (not him).'

6–8] May he be scorned by some woman who is scorned by all other men, and may he have to deny on oath to others that he has said the things he has said to her, being torn between the fear of failing to win her, and the shame of doing so.

9–10] May he turn his sorrow into madness, and his cramp into gout, by merely remembering who it is that has given him them.

11–13] And may he feel no twinge of conscience at having seduced her, but only of remorse at his loss of reputation, and may he be racked by the thought, not that he has committed a sin, but that *she* was the woman he made love to.

14 *scarceness*] poverty.

15–16] For land which he would have inherited if his adulterous connexion with a near kinswoman had not interposed an heir between himself and the estate.

19] i.e. so that he may not recover his reputation posthumously.

22–3] Or may he feed parasites for so long that he drains himself dry, and would wish to sponge on them in his turn.

24] A difficult line. I suggest that it may mean: 'And in the end turn Jew so as to keep alive' (alluding to mutual assistance within the Jewish community). The line might owe something to Gen. xxxiv. 22-3.

29 *And all*] I preserve the capital 'A' here as almost certainly intended to imitate the form of a legal document.

THE MESSAGE

Send home my long-stray'd eyes to me,
Which, oh too long, have dwelt on thee;
Yet since there they have learn'd such ill,
    Such forc'd fashions,
    And false passions,
      That they be
      Made by thee
Fit for no good sight, keep them still.

Send home my harmless heart again,
Which no unworthy thought could stain;
But if it be taught by thine
    To make jestings
    Of protestings,
      And cross both
      Word and oath,
Keep it, for then 'tis none of mine.

Yet send me back my heart and eyes,
That I may know, and see, thy lies,
And may laugh and joy, when thou
    Art in anguish
    And dost languish
      For some one
      That will none,
Or prove as false as thou art now.

THE MESSAGE

3 *learn'd*] became acquainted with.

3–4] *such ill, Such forc'd fashions*] such affected habits. (As Mr Ingram has suggested to me, the association of fantastically stuffed garments, belying the form beneath, is probably present in the phrase.)

8 *Fit for no good sight*] possibly 'no longer able to tell' (or 'appreciate') 'genuineness if they saw it.'

14 *cross*] literally 'cancel' (Grierson), or possibly 'contravene'. Both senses were current in Donne's day (see *O.E.D.*). There is not much to choose between them in the present context, and 'break' would probably be the best modern equivalent.

23 *That will none*] probably: 'that will have no truck with you'.

A NOCTURNAL UPON ST LUCY'S DAY; BEING THE SHORTEST DAY

'Tis the year's midnight, and it is the day's,
Lucy's, who scarce seven hours herself unmasks;
  The sun is spent, and now his flasks
  Send forth light squibs, no constant rays;
    The world's whole sap is sunk;
The general balm the hydroptic earth hath drunk,
Whither, as to the bed's-feet, life is shrunk,
Dead and interr'd; yet all these seem to laugh,
Compar'd with me, who am their epitaph.

Study me then, you who shall lovers be
At the next world, that is, at the next Spring:
  For I am every dead thing,
  In whom love wrought new alchemy.
    For his art did express
A quíntessence even from nothingness,
From dull privations, and lean emptiness:
He ruin'd me, and I am re-begot
Of absence, darkness, death; things which are not.

All others, from all things, draw all that's good,
Life, soul, form, spirit, whence they being have;
  I, by Love's limbeck, am the grave
  Of all that's nothing. Oft a flood
    Have we two wept, and so
Drown'd the whole world, us two; oft did we grow
To be two Chaoses, when we did show
Care to aught else; and often absences
Withdrew our souls, and made us carcases.

But I am by her death (which word wrongs her),
Of the first nothing the Elixir grown;
  Were I a man, that I were one
  I needs must know; I should prefer,
    If I were any beast,

A NOCTURNAL UPON ST LUCY'S DAY

General Note: There is controversy as to the person to whom this poem refers. It may refer to Lucy, Countess of Bedford. If it does, it was perhaps written in the time of an illness of hers, when she was at the point of death in 1612. It is interesting to note that the atmosphere of the poem is rather similar to that of the beginning of the poem which Donne wrote on the death of the Countess's brother, Lord Harrington (*Obsequies to the Lord Harrington*) (see especially ll. 15 ff. of that poem). Lord Harrington died at his sister's house at Twickenham early in 1614.

Mr J. B. Leishman, in his book on Donne, *The Monarch of Wit*, Hutchinson, 1951, takes a different view. He raises the possibility that the poem may have been written by Donne to his wife during some grave illness, e.g. in 1611. In favour of this view he cites the resemblance (which had also struck me before I read Mr Leishman's book) between *A Valediction: of weeping* and the third stanza of the *Nocturnal*, and suggests that the *Nocturnal* is much more like the poems certainly or probably written to Donne's wife than to 'the Platonic or Courtly poems'. In my own opinion, however, it is a mistake to call all the poems addressed to the Countess of Bedford 'Platonic or Courtly': those epithets do not fit *Twickenham Garden*, for instance, which was very probably addressed to the Countess of Bedford.

There is also the possibility that the poem may refer to the death of Donne's wife in 1617.

The controversy certainly cannot be regarded as settled. On the one hand the use of the word 'Lucy' is striking: though not conclusive. On the other hand, the content of the poem shows that a relationship of great and tempestuous intimacy lies behind it. That is, however, not conclusive evidence in favour of the view that the poem is about Donne's wife. It is hard to say how intimate Donne's relationship with the Countess of Bedford had become by 1612. (*Twickenham Garden* was probably written in or before 1609.)

2 *Lucy's*] St Lucy's Day, 13 December, evidently believed by Donne to be the 'shortest day in the year' in the old Julian calendar, used in England in Donne's time, and indeed until 1752. (According to Professor Garrod, on the authority of Professor Plaskett, that day was never in actual fact the shortest in any year during Donne's life time. (*Donne, Poetry and Prose*, Clarendon Press, 1946.))

3 *flasks*] powder-horns.

4 *squibs*] Mr T. R. Henn has pointed out to me that this term was used for the half-charges on which military recruits were practised.

6] 'the hydroptic earth' is, of course, the subject of this clause.

general balm] possibly meaning the general aromatic fragrance of nature, which subsides with the fall of the sap the earth has 'drunk', rather than specifically the resin and volatile oils of the genus Balsamodendron. But possibly there is a play on the aromatic ointment made from these, and used for soothing pain and healing wounds. (1563: T. Gale: 'The Balm wherewith green and fresh wounds are

Some ends, some means; yea plants, yea stones, detest,
And love; all, all, some properties invest;
If I an ordinary nothing were,
As shadow, a light and body must be here.

But I am none; nor will my Sun renew.
You lovers, for whose sake the lesser sun
At this time to the Goat is run
To fetch new lust, and give it you,
Enjoy your summer all:
Since she enjoys her long night's festival,
Let me prepare towards her, and let me call
This hour her Vigil, and her Eve, since this
Both the year's, and the day's, deep midnight is.

---

speedily cured' (*O.E.D.*).) The suggestion would then be that there is no comfort for grief. Another possibility is that 'balm' is here used in the Paracelsian sense of 'preservative vital essence'. I am, however, strongly tempted by a possibility suggested to me by Mr Ingram, namely, that the 'general balm' may itself *be* the sap (which is, in any case, what the earth has 'drunk'). Acquaintance with particular cases of the use of the term 'balm' around Donne's time has given me the impression that *some* writers, at least, thought that balm was the actual sap of certain plants. In that case, why should not 'general balm' mean all the sap of all plants?

hydroptic] dropsical, and therefore insatiably thirsty (cf. Donne's letter to Sir Henry Goodyer (September 1608): 'An hydroptique immoderate desire of humane learning and languages').

7 *bed's feet*] I think this should be taken to mean the foot of the bed rather than the four feet of the four-poster bedstead. The image is probably that of a dying man whose life has ebbed away to his feet, and therefore to the foot of the bed. Some cases of death can be plausibly conceived in that way.

12 *every*] A difficult textual point. I tentatively follow Grierson here in adopting the reading of the 1633 edition and of a number of the MSS, in preference to the reading of the 1635–69 editions 'a very', adopted by Chambers. The reading 'every' seems to me to be supported internally by the sense of ll. 21–2.

12–18] A hard passage. I suggest that the sense is as follows: 'For I am made of everything dead, and Love transmuted me by a new chemical process: for he managed to extract' (express = squeeze out) 'a quintessence even from nothingness, from melancholy absences and starvation (of desires ?). He completely destroyed me, and then begot me again out of absence, darkness and death, things which don't exist.'

15 *quintessence*] the 'fifth essence' of ancient and medieval philosophy, supposed to be the substance of which the heavenly bodies were composed, and to be actually latent in all things. The extraction of it by distillation and other methods was one of the great objects of alchemy.

16 *emptiness:*] This is the reading of 1719, followed by Grierson (emptiness 1633–54; emptiness, 1669). I think it is probably preferable to the absence of a stop, since to take l. 16 with l. 17 requires forced construction of 'From' in l. 16.

17 *ruin'd*] ? 'destroyed' (*O.E.D.* (obsolete)). (*O.E.D.* quotes 1621. Burton: 'He fell down dead upon the Dragon, & killed him with the fall, so both were ruin'd'. 1645. Symonds's Diary: 'Cromwell's horse & dragoons ruined some of our horse that quartered about Islip'.)

19–22] Everyone else but me draws everything good out of other things. They acquire from them life, soul, form, and spirit, which are what give them their being. I, however, through the trick of Love's chemistry, am simply the burial-ground of everything that doesn't exist.

21 *limbeck*] alembic, a primitive form of retort.

24 *us two*] i.e. we were the whole world (cf. perhaps *The Good-morrow*, ll. 10–14).

25–6 *when we did show Care to aught else*] probably 'when either of us made the other jealous by showing an inclination for someone or something else'.

28–9] Continuing the allusions to cosmic events such as the Creation and the Flood, made in the latter part of the preceding stanza, Donne now says that an even more immense and extraordinary thing has taken place in him, through the death of his lady, than anything that occurred to them both while she was alive, namely, that he has become the quintessence (Elixir here = quintessence) of the *first* Nothing, which subsisted before the Creation of the world, and out of which the world was created.

31–3 *I should prefer . . . means*] If I were a lower animal of some sort I should at least have the characteristic of having preferences as to objectives and as to the means of attaining them.

33 *yea stones, detest*] Grierson quotes a passage from one of Donne's Sermons, in which Donne says that stones may have life. Cf. the later systematic philosophy of Leibniz's *Monadology*.

34 *all, all, some properties invest*] absolutely everything is endowed with *some* properties.

35] He is the quintessence of the first Nothing, which, unlike an 'ordinary' nothing, does not imply the existence of anything else.

36 *As*] such as.

36] i.e. as he is the quintessence of the first Nothing, neither light nor body exist, and therefore shadows cannot be cast.

37 *my Sun*] i.e. his dead lady, whose beams will never shine on him again on earth.

38 *the lesser sun*] i.e. the sun.

39 *the Goat*] This can be taken to mean either the Tropic of Capricorn or the zodiacal sign of Capricorn. It does not much matter which; for the sun enters the sign of Capricorn about 22 December (or 12 December in the old Julian calendar): and, likewise, at roughly the same time it shines perpendicularly over the Tropic of Capricorn, the farthest limit of its journey into the Southern Hemisphere. (Cf. *The Progresse of the Soule*, 336–7, and *The First Anniversarie*, 263–7.)

40] the goat being notoriously the most lustful of animals.

42 *she*] i.e. his dead beloved.

her long night's festival] both (1) the long sleep of death (cf. Catullus's

> Nobis cum semel occidit brevis lux
> nox est perpetua una dormienda);

and (2) her resurrection (cf. Donne's Sermon on 1 Cor. xv. 26. *The last Enemy that shall be destroyed, is Death*: 'This is a text of the resurrection, and it is not Easter yet; but it is Easter eve; all Lent is but the vigil, the eve of Easter: to so long a festival as shall never end, the resurrection, we may well begin the eve betimes.' (Works, ed. Alford, I, p. 233.)

43 *Let me prepare towards her*] probably meaning primarily 'Let me prepare myself devotionally' (as would an intending Easter communicant) 'as a participant' (or even ? 'ministrant') 'in the celebration of her festival.' This would also naturally imply that he wishes to share in her death and resurrection. I am much indebted to Mr Ingram for his help in arriving at this explanation.

44 *Vigil*] service used on the night before a holiday or festival, but there is possibly also a reference here to a devotional watch over a dead body.

42–5] The hour is especially appropriate to his loss and grief, and also to her eternal festival, for it is the deepest midnight there is—the midnight of the longest night of the year.

WITCHCRAFT BY A PICTURE

I fix mine eye on thine, and there
  Pity my picture burning in thine eye;
My picture drown'd in a transparent tear
  When I look lower I espy;
    Hadst thou the wicked skill
By pictures made and marr'd, to kill,
How many ways mightst thou perform thy will!

But now I have drunk thy sweet salt tears;
  And though thou pour more I'll depart:
My picture vanish'd, vanish fears
  That I can be endamag'd by that art;
    Though thou retain of me
One picture more, yet that will be,
Being in thine own heart, from all malice free.

WITCHCRAFT BY A PICTURE

6] to kill people by making pictures of them, and then destroying the pictures. (One reputed method of witchcraft. For another reference by Donne to the device see *Sermons*, ed. Potter and Simpson, I. 160.)

7 *!*] In the seventeenth-century editions this appears as a '*?*', a common typographical equivalent at the time for a mark of exclamation.

14 *from all malice free*] This is possibly a tender joke on Donne's part. The sense seems on the surface to be that her heart is so free from malice that nothing lodged there could come to harm: but Donne may also intend the sense that his lady will not attack that picture, simply because to do so would be to attack her own heart.

THE BAIT

Come live with me, and be my love,
And we will some new pleasures prove
Of golden sands, and crystal brooks:
With silken lines, and silver hooks.

There will the river whispering run
Warm'd by thy eyes, more than the Sun;
And there the enamour'd fish will stay,
Begging themselves they may betray.

When thou wilt swim in that live bath,
Each fish, which every channel hath,
Will amorously to thee swim,
Gladder to catch thee, than thou him.

If thou to be so seen be'st loath
By Sun, or Moon, thou dark'nest both,
And if myself have leave to see,
I need not their light, having thee.

Let others freeze with angling reeds,
And cut their legs with shells and weeds,
Or treacherously poor fish beset,
With strangling snare, or windowy net:

Let coarse bold hands, from slimy nest
The bedded fish in banks out-wrest;
Or curious traitors, sleave-silk flies,
Bewitch poor fishes' wand'ring eyes.

For thee, thou need'st no such deceit,
For thou thyself art thine own bait;
That fish, that is not catch'd thereby,
Alas, is wiser far than I.

THE BAIT

General Note: A sequel to Marlowe's *Come live with me, and be my love.* Walton, in *The Compleat Angler*, where Donne's poem is quoted, makes one of the characters say that the poem was made by Donne to show the world that he could write softly and smoothly when he wanted to.

3 :] I have strengthened the comma of the seventeenth-century editions, because I think it possible that Donne intended l. 4 as a sharp recoil from the trend of Marlowe's poem.

8 *Begging*] i.e. begging that.

17 *reeds*] rods.

23 *sleave-silk*] 'made from sleave-silk', which is defined by *O.E.D.* as 'silk thread capable of being separated into smaller filaments for use in embroidery, etc.'

THE APPARITION

When by thy scorn, O murd'ress, I am dead,
    And that thou thinkst thee free
From all solicitation from me,
Then shall my ghost come to thy bed,
And thee, feign'd vestal, in worse arms shall see;
Then thy sick taper will begin to wink,
And he, whose thou art then, being tir'd before,
Will, if thou stir, or pinch to wake him, think
    Thou call'st for more,
And in false sleep will from thee shrink;
And then, poor aspen wretch, neglected thou
Bath'd in a cold quicksilver sweat wilt lie,
    A verier ghost than I:
What I will say, I will not tell thee now,
Lest that preserve thee; and since my love is spent,
I had rather thou shouldst painfully repent,
Than by my threat'nings rest still innocent.

THE APPARITION

3 *solicitation*] '-ation' trisyllabic.

6 *wink*] grow dim or flicker before going out.

12 *quicksilver*] so accented even as late as Johnson's time (see his *Dictionary*). The accentuation has not been unheard in the present century—e.g. in the music-hall song:

I've often said to myself, I've said:
'Cheer up, Quicksilver, you'll soon be dead;
It's a short life and a gay one!'

THE BROKEN HEART

He is stark mad, who ever says
  That he hath been in love an hour;
Yet not that love so soon decays,
  But that it can ten in less space devour:
Who will believe me, if I swear
That I have had the plague a year?
  Who would not laugh at me, if I should say
  I saw a flask of powder burn a day?

Ah, what a trifle is a heart,
  If once into love's hands it come!
All other griefs allow a part
  To other griefs, and ask themselves but some;
They come to us, but us Love draws,
He swallows us, and never chaws:
  By him, as by chain'd shot, whole ranks do die;
  He is the tyrant pike, our hearts the fry.

If 'twere not so, what did become
  Of my heart, when I first saw thee?
I brought a heart into the room,
  But from the room I carried none with me:
If it had gone to thee, I know
Mine would have taught thine heart to show
  More pity unto me: but Love, alas,
  At one fierce blow did shiver it as glass.

Yet nothing can to nothing fall,
  Nor any place be empty quite,
Therefore I think my breast hath all
  Those pieces still, though they be not unite;
And now, as broken glasses show
A hundred lesser faces, so
  My rags of heart can like, wish, and adore,
  But after one such love, can love no more.

8 *flask of powder*] This is the reading of the 1633 edition, and of many MSS. A number of other MSS, however, including some of high authority, read 'flash'. In support of 'flask', Grierson quotes a parallel from *Romeo and Juliet*, III. iii. 130:

> Thy wit, that ornament to shape and love,
> Mis-shapen in the conduct of them both:
> Like powder in a skilless soldier's flaske,
> Is set a fire by thine own ignorance,
> And thou dismembred with thine owne defence.

The 'flask' was a powder-horn.

14 *chaws*] chews.

15 *chain'd shot*] cannon balls or half-balls chained together, which normally separated in flight to chain length, and could cut down whole ranks of men.

16 *fry*] swarm of small fish, forming the pike's prey.

24 *At one fierce blow*] After some hesitation I have decided to follow here the reading of an important group of MSS which may contain corrections by Donne: in preference to the reading 'at one first blow' found in other MSS and in the printed editions, and followed by Grierson. My chief reason is that 'at one first blow' is redundant, and that I believe that such redundancy might well have led to correction on the part of Donne. 'Fierce', moreover, gives a stronger tone to the line and a more vivid impression of Love's actions.

24] with the result that his heart never reached his lady.

25] alluding to the belief that matter is indestructible.

26] alluding to the belief that an absolute vacuum is impossible.

29 *glasses*] mirrors.

31–2] The sense comes out most clearly if the words 'like', 'wish', 'adore', and the two words 'love' in the last line, are emphasized.

A VALEDICTION: FORBIDDING MOURNING

As virtuous men pass mildly away,
   And whisper to their souls, to go,
Whilst some of their sad friends do say:
   'The breath goes now', and some say: 'No':

So let us melt, and make no noise,
   No tear-floods, nor sigh-tempests move;
'Twere profanation of our joys
   To tell the laity our love.

Moving of the earth brings harms and fears;
   Men reckon what it did and meant:
But trepidation of the spheres,
   Though greater far, is innocent.

Dull súblunary lovers' love
   (Whose soul is sense) cannot admit
Absence, because it doth remove
   Those things which elemented it.

But we, by a love so much refin'd
   That our selves know not what it is,
Inter-assurèd of the mind,
   Care less, eyes, lips, and hands to miss.

Our two souls therefore, which are one,
   Though I must go, endure not yet
A breach, but an expansion,
   Like gold to airy thinness beat.

If they be two, they are two so
   As stiff twin compasses are two:
Thy soul, the fix'd foot, makes no show
   To move, but doth, if the other do;

A VALEDICTION: FORBIDDING MOURNING

General Note: This poem is quoted (though with some variations from the earlier texts) in Walton's *Life of Donne*. (Chambers points out that it was not printed in the first three editions of the *Life*.) Walton says that the lines were given by Donne to his wife when he left her to go with Sir Robert Drury to France in 1611. Walton adds: 'And I beg leave to tell, that I have heard some Criticks, learned, both in Languages and Poetry, say, that none of the Greek or Latin Poets did ever equal them.'

6 *move*] stir up.

7 *profanation*] The primary sense in English is quite certainly religious = 'desecration of something sacred'. 'By extension' (*O.E.D.*): 'the degradation or vulgarization of anything worthy of being held in reverence or respect'. *O.E.D.* cites this passage from Donne as an instance of the extended meaning. There is, however, certainly more to it than this. By this word and the word 'laity' in l. 8, I think Donne almost certainly wishes to allude to love as a mystery or cult, with adepts or initiates such as himself and his wife (to whom the poem was written). This idea certainly occurs in a number of places in Donne, for instance in: 'We for Love's clergy only are instruments' in *A Valediction: of the book* (l. 22) (see notes on that poem).

9 *Moving of the earth*] an earth-quake.
brings] causes.

10] Not such an easy line as it might look. I think the meaning is: 'People calculate the damage it has done, and try to estimate its significance.' (An alternative interpretation is that it means: 'people narrate, etc.': but this older use of 'reckon' was fast dying out at the end of the sixteenth century. *O.E.D.* give no instance after 1586.) Despite the scientific explanations of earthquakes given by Aristotle and others, and supported by later medieval theologians (e.g. the Cardinal d'Ailly, in *Concordia astronomicae veritatis cum Theologia*, Paris, 1483), earthquakes were still generally regarded as evidence of the wrath of God.

11] At the date when the poem was written there were three current senses of the word 'trepidation': (1) was 'tremulous agitation' (applying to persons); (2) was 'tremor' (applying to things); (3) was the astronomical sense, which *O.E.D.* describes as follows: 'A libration of the eighth (or ninth) sphere, added to the system of Ptolemy by the Arab astronomer Thabet ben Korrah, *c.* 950, in order to account for certain phenomena, especially precession, really due to motion of the earth's axis.' This libration (oscillation) would communicate itself to all the smaller spheres. It was harmless ('innocent' in l. 12 meaning 'harmless'), in the sense that no harmful effect or portentous significance had ever been attributed to it.

13 *sublunary*] 'earthly', and therefore inferior, and moreover, subject to change like everything below the moon in medieval cosmology: but the literal meaning of 'sublunary' also suggests, as Mr T. R. Henn has pointed out (in *The Apple and the Spectroscope*, p. 22), that such lovers are subject to ebb and flow like the tides. Although an accurate detailed

And though it in the centre sit,
  Yet when the other far doth roam,
It leans, and hearkens after it,
  And grows erect, as that comes home.

Such wilt thou be to me, who must,
  Like the other foot, obliquely run:
Thy firmness makes my circle just,
  And makes me end where I begun.

account of the forces governing the tides was not given before Newton, correlation between the phases of the moon and the tides had often been made even in ancient times (e.g. by Strabo, Posidonius, Pliny) and it continued to be made in medieval times (see Dante) and in the Renaissance (e.g. by Kepler, whose work Donne knew).

14 (*Whose soul is sense*)] 'whose whole essence is sensuality;' or possibly, as Mr Henn has suggested to me, 'whose souls depend on the properties of sensation'.

admit] we would now say, perhaps, 'stand'.

16 *elemented it*] 'were the elements of which it (sublunary love) was made'. 'Composed it' would be rather a loose translation (cf. a passage from Donne's *LXXX Sermons*, XLVIII. 487: 'Elemented and composed of heresies' (i.e. so that all the parts and even the least parts (the elements) were heresies).

19 *Inter-assurèd of the mind*] 'mutually confident of the fidelity of each other's minds'; but probably 'inter-assurèd' also contains a reference to a solemn legal assurance, or transference of title.

22 *endure not yet*] nevertheless do not suffer.

23 *expansion*] to be pronounced as four syllables.

24] Alluding, of course, to the beating of gold into leaf. Mr Henn has suggested to me that there may be a further allusion here: to the airy thinness of the bodies assumed by angels (cf. *Air and Angels*). Mr Ingram calls my attention also to the fact that one ounce of gold, beaten out to the present standard thickness of English gold leaf (1/250,000 in.), would cover an area of 250 sq. ft.

25] As Grierson has pointed out, a simile based on the pair of compasses had already appeared in Omar Khayyam (see op. cit., II. 41). Another instance occurs in one of Guarini's madrigals (No. XCVI, *Rime*, Venice, 1598), as Professor Praz has indicated (*Secentismo e Marinismo in Inghilterra*, 1925, p. 109, note): and Hall had also used such a simile in a poem printed in 1609, over two years before Donne wrote this poem. (See Professor F. P. Wilson, *Elizabethan and Jacobean*, p. 30.)

31 *hearkens*] probably intended to suggest the forward-leaning posture of a listener.

32 *that*] the other foot.

32, 36] What do these lines refer to? There are several views current: (1) That they both refer to the completion of the circle; (2) that they both refer to the closing of the compasses; (3) that l. 32 refers to the closing of the compasses, while l. 36 refers to the completion of the circle. I feel fairly convinced that l. 36, at any rate, refers to the completion of the circle, and that view (2) is therefore wrong. It would seem strange to say that the 'firmness' of the fixed foot makes the moving foot end up next to the fixed foot when the compasses are closed. Furthermore, there is evidence from phraseology in Donne's use elsewhere of the image of a pair of compasses or the description of a circle, that l. 36 refers to the completion of the circle. Mr Josef

Lederer has, for another purpose, collected cases of Donne's use of the simile of a pair of compasses (see Mr Lederer's interesting article 'John Donne and the Emblematic Practice' in *The Review of English Studies*, July 1946). In one of the passages he quotes (from *Fifty Sermons*, London, 1649, I. 3) Donne writes: 'The Body of Man was the first point that the foot of God's Compasse was upon: First he created the Body of *Adam*: then he carries his Compasse round, and shuts up where he began, he ends with the Body of Man againe in the glorification thereof in the Resurrection.' Here Donne actually uses a phrase 'shuts up where he began', which, even more strongly than 'makes me end where I begun', would in itself suggest the closing of the compasses; and yet, in this passage from the sermon, it clearly refers to the completion of the circle, not to the closing of the compasses. Mr Adrian Cohen, of Jesus College, has drawn my attention to another case of similar phraseology referring clearly to the completion of a circle, viz. ll. 275–6 of *The First Anniversary*:

So, of the Starres that boast that they do runne
In Circle still, none ends where he begun.

All this seems to point to l. 36 referring to the completion of the circle.

As to views (1) and (3), after some hesitation I incline to view (3). I think l. 32 more probably refers to the closing of the compasses, first, because the fixed leg does not strictly 'grow erect' (i.e. grow erect in all planes) at any time during the description of the circle; and secondly, because the expression 'comes home' seems clearly intended to contrast with 'far doth roam', and this latter phrase seems more naturally to refer to the distance between the feet than to the distance along the circumference from the starting-point of the description of a circle.

I feel bound to add that if view (3) is correct, as seems probable, then, despite the fact that the circle was for Donne (as for so many Medieval and Renaissance writers) the symbol of perfection, and despite also the fact that drawing circles, rather than being closed, is the special function of compasses, the ending of the poem is to me not wholly satisfying, since the completion of the circle is somewhat of an anticlimax as a symbol of homecoming after the symbol of the closing of the compasses.

34 *obliquely run*] After some thought I feel convinced that this simply refers to the fact that the describing arm follows a curved path, not a straight line.

35 *makes*] The reading of one of the MSS (British Museum, Sloane MS 1792) is 'draws'. Mr John Hayward, who first printed it in the Nonesuch Donne, said that it also occurred in a seventeenth-century commonplace book belonging to Mr John Sparrow. The reading of the old printed editions and of the other MSS is 'makes'. At first sight, 'draws' is a more attractive reading than 'makes'; but it has its own

disadvantages. First, it might be said, the fixed foot does not *draw* the circle. Secondly, the phrase 'to draw just' is rather unsatisfactory. On the other hand, 'draws' is less tame than 'makes', and also avoids the repetition; and, further, it suggests in a lively way the process of drawing. Moreover, it is only a stretch complimentary to the woman to say that if it causes the circle to be drawn perfectly, it in a sense 'draws' it. Finally, it involves a valuable suggestion of the attractive force which the woman exerts on the man. (Cf. the primary tractive meaning of 'draw', which is also, perhaps, present here in a reference to the centripetal force controlling the moving foot of the compasses.) On balance, therefore, despite the overwhelming weight of textual authority against it, it seems to me the better of two not altogether satisfactory words. After much hesitation, however, I have decided not to print 'draws', since not only is the amount of evidence for it slight, but Sloane MS 1792 is not an impressive MS.

THE ECSTASY

Where, like a pillow on a bed,
  A pregnant bank swell'd up, to rest
The violet's reclining head,
  Sat we two, one another's best.

Our hands were firmly cémented
  With a fast balm, which thence did spring;
Our eye-beams twisted, and did thread
  Our eyes, upon one double string:

So to intergraft our hands, as yet
  Was all the means to make us one,
And pictures on our eyes to get
  Was all our propagation.

As, 'twixt two equal armies, Fate
  Suspends uncertain victory,
Our souls (which to advance their state
  Were gone out) hung 'twixt her, and me.

And whilst our souls negotiate there,
  We like sepulchral statues lay;
All day, the same our postures were,
  And we said nothing, all the day.

If any, so by love refin'd
  That he souls' language understood,
And by good love were grown all mind,
  Within convenient distance stood,

He (though he knew not which soul spake,
  Because both meant, both spake the same)
Might thence a new concoction take,
  And part far purer than he came.

THE ECSTASY

Note on the printing of the poem: Many of the MSS divided the poem into quatrains. The 1633 editor, who was perhaps the printer, did not preserve this division, but printed the poem in one continuous block. This practice has been followed by subsequent editors with the honourable exception of Chambers. In my view, this is a bad old tradition. I believe it has even contributed to the difficulty of understanding the poem. It has certainly made the poem needlessly and inelegantly ponderous in appearance.
General Note on the title: After careful consideration I feel convinced that the overwhelmingly predominant meaning of this title is the mystical state in which a soul, liberated from the body, contemplates divine truths. The souls of the lovers in this poem communicate their thoughts in this state to the understanding listener.

5 *cémented*] so accented in Donne's time.
6 *fast*] i.e. set fast.
balm] here simply meaning an aromatic resinous exudation.
9 *So*] either (1) in that way; or (2) therefore.
intergraft] ('entergraft' in the originals. The prefix 'enter-' already gave ground to 'inter-' in the seventeenth century, and now barely survives.) It is doubtful whether Donne meant 'intergraft' to be taken in a strict horticultural way. In any case, no such two-way flow of sap as he would need for a perfect horticultural image would result from any known process of grafting. Probably, therefore, the term 'intergraft' should be taken in a general figurative meaning: 'fix in each other so as to produce a vital union'.
11 *on*] I have ventured to adopt this vivid reading of a large number of MSS in preference to the tamer 'in' of the 1633–69 editions.
get] beget.
12 *propagation*] to be pronounced as five syllables.
13–17] The situation described is somewhat obscure. Mr F. L. Lucas has suggested to me that there may be some reminiscence of Homer's Zeus holding the scales with the fates of Hector and Achilles, in *Iliad*, XXII. 209 ff. Donne would certainly be familiar with this situation through the passage in *Aeneid*, XII. 725–7, where Virgil imitates the Homeric lines. Ll. 13–17 of Donne's poem, however, taken together, seem to give a more active role to the two souls than that of mere destinies which are to be weighed. They seem at least to be *parleying* from their scale-pans, if they are still there by l. 17.
27 *concoction*] a purification or sublimation by heat, e.g. of metals in a furnace. According to a common belief at that time, the heat from the sun 'concocted' gold below the earth's surface. (Cf. Donne's *Sermons*, ed. Potter and Simpson, I. 163, 272.)
32] We can see that we did not see before what the cause of our love was (cf. *A Valediction: forbidding mourning*, l. 18).
33 *several*] separate.
36 *each this and that*] A somewhat obscure phrase, possibly meaning that there is no distinction of 'this' and 'that' between the two souls once

'This Ecstasy doth unperplex,'
We said, 'and tell us what we love;
We see by this it was not sex;
We see we saw not what did move:

'But as all several souls contain
Mixture of things, they know not what,
Love these mix'd souls doth mix again,
And makes both one, each this and that.

'A single violet transplant,—
The strength, the colour, and the size,
All which before was poor, and scant,
Redoubles still, and multiplies.

'When love, with one another so
Interinanimates two souls,
That abler soul, which thence doth flow,
Defects of loneliness controls.

'We then, who are this new soul, know
Of what we are compos'd, and made,
For the atomies of which we grow,
Are souls, whom no change can invade.

'But oh alas, so long, so far
Our bodies why do we forbear?
They are ours, though they are not we, we are
The intelligences, they the sphere.

'We owe them thanks, because they thus
Did us, to us, at first convey,
Yielded their forces, sense, to us,
Nor are dross to us, but allay.

'On man heaven's influence works not so,
But that it first imprints the air;
So soul into the soul may flow,
Though it to body first repair.

love has united them, so that each can equally well be called 'this' or 'that': alternatively, the meaning may be that by the working of love the two souls become qualitatively indistinguishable, both now consisting of precisely the same mixture of elements. The second interpretation seems to me the more probable.

37 *A single violet transplant*] This seems a point additional to what has gone before. It foreshadows the point of ll. 41–4, viz. that by 'interinanimation' the two souls grow, as well as being mixed. The working of the image is not, however, clear. Nothing corresponds to the other soul in the case of the violet.

—] I have supplied the dash to make clear that ll. 38–40 are to be taken together, and that 'violet' is not the subject of l. 40.

39] I have removed the parentheses from round this line for the same reasons. ('All which' = 'All of which').

41–2] ? paralleling 'intergraft' (i. 9).

42] uses two souls to give a quickening of life to each other.

44] restrains the defects which the two separate souls had before union.

41–4] The process described in these lines is not clear. There seem at least two possible interpretations: (1) that the two souls are united to form one soul; (2) that the two souls are not actually united, but an oversoul comes into being as a result of their 'interinanimation'. Some support is lent to interpretation (2) by the plural 'intelligences' in l. 52: but interpretation (1) seems in closer accord with ll. 33–48. This may be another instance of the uncertainty referred to in my note on l. 14 of *The Good-morrow*.

47 *atomies*] atoms.

51 *we are . . . sphere*] i.e. we are related to our bodies as angels are related to the sphere they control. In the Christianized Ptolemaic astronomy, various orders of angels each ruled one of the spheres from the moon's (which was the first) sphere to the crystalline (or ninth) sphere. Grierson here adopted this reading of all the MSS in preference to the reading of all the printed editions 1633–69: 'spheres'. In support of his choice he says: 'The bodies made one are the Sphere in which the two Intelligences meet and command.' 'Sphere' is also far preferable on the score of rhyme, though, as Grierson points out, Donne does elsewhere rhyme a word ending in 's' with a word not ending in 's'. Whatever the correct interpretation of ll. 41–4, it is clear that in l. 51 Donne is not treating the two 'intelligences' as unified. He may be starting again from scratch here. By the use of the singular 'sphere' here Donne *may possibly* be trying to *suggest* to his mistress the physical union he wishes to achieve with her.

55] I wholeheartedly follow Grierson in preferring the reading of all the MSS, 'forces, sense' to 'senses force', the reading of the printed editions 1633–69. After the privilege of discussion with him, I am moreover convinced that he is probably right in explaining 'forces, sense' to

'As our blood labours to beget
    Spirits, as like souls as it can,
Because such fingers need to knit
    That subtle knot, which makes us man:

'So must pure lovers' souls descend
    To affections, and to faculties,
Which sense may reach and apprehend,
    Else a great Prince in prison lies.

'To our bodies turn we then, that so
    Weak men on love reveal'd may look;
Love's mysteries in souls do grow,
    But yet the body is his book:

'And if some lover, such as we,
    Have heard this dialogue of one,
Let him still mark us, he shall see
    Small change, when we are to bodies gone.'

---

mean 'their forces, namely sense', in distinction from the mental forces of the soul.

56 *dross*] the scum of molten metals, which is a waste product.
allay] 'The metal of a baser kind mixed in coins to harden them, that they may wear less' (Dr Johnson's Dictionary). The modern form of the word is, of course, 'alloy'.

53–6] These lines epitomize the philosophy of combined spiritual and physical love which underlies this poem.

57–8] i.e. the planets and stars can only exert their influences on man by first affecting the air. Grierson quotes a passage from Du Bartas dated 1581, which refers to Pliny's *Natural History*, Plutarch, Plato, and Aristotle, for opinions on the point.

59–60] In Scholastic cosmology the planets and stars were considered to be guided by intelligences which were superior to human souls. In a sense, therefore, 'heaven's influence' on man was the influence of one spiritual substance on another. This fact reveals the parallel with the interaction of human souls through the medium of body.

Grierson points out that Aquinas himself did not accept the view that intelligences act on man mediately and controllingly. He considered that they illuminated the human intellect without influencing the will. (Grierson, II. 44; cf. Aquinas, *Summa Theol.*, I. cxv. 4.) It seems to me, then, more natural to suppose that Donne was not referring here to Aquinas's distinction, which would blur his point.

60 *repair*] goes to.

61–4] 'Spirits' were thought of as a thin vapour or rarefied liquid, very active in character, either extracted from the blood or a thin part of it, which acted on the soul to produce sensations, and was used by the soul to perform bodily actions. There were various kinds of 'spirits', according to the part of the body in which they had their origin. A clear account of 'spirits' appears in Descartes in the *Principia* and in the *Traité des Passions*. Professor Grierson quotes a passage from Burton's *Anatomy of Melancholy* (1638), in which it is stated that 'spirits' were currently held either to form a *medium* between soul and body, or, as by Paracelsus, to constitute a fourth soul.

63–4] 'Because such almost immaterial fingers are needed to tie that extremely complex and elusive knot, holding body and soul together, which makes us into human beings with all our human functions.' (Descartes thought the knot was tied in the pineal gland.) There is a strikingly parallel passage to the whole quatrain, in one of Donne's *Sermons*: 'In our naturall persons, the body and soul do not make a perfect man, except they be united, except our spirits (which are the active part of the blood) do fit this body and soule for one another's working.' (ed. Potter and Simpson, VI. 128.)

66 *affections*] passions.

faculties] here probably powers of action, as contrasted with passions.

67] within the range of the senses.

68 *a great Prince*] probably Love, or else, as Grierson has suggested to me, the soul, which has capacity to love.

70 *Weak men*] i.e. men who are unable to sustain their faith in love without some outward manifestation of its mysteries.

74 *of one*] Not, I think, 'from somebody', but a paradoxical phrase referring to the fact that the two souls were speaking as one.

75–6] i.e. our love will still have much the same height and depth as it had before.

76 *when we are*] even when we *are*.

LOVE'S DEITY

I long to talk with some old lover's ghost,
  Who died before the God of Love was born:
I cannot think that he who then lov'd most
  Sunk so low as to love one which did scorn.
But since this god produc'd a destiny,
And that vice-nature, custom, lets it be:
  I must love her, that loves not me.

Sure, they which made him god, meant not so much;
  Nor he, in his young godhead, practis'd it:
But when an even flame two hearts did touch,
  His office was indulgently to fit
Actives to passives. Correspondency
Only his subject was; it cannot be
  Love, till I love her that loves me.

But every modern god will now extend
  His vast prerogative, as far as Jove.
To rage, to lust, to write to, to commend,
  All is the purlieu of the God of Love.
Oh! were we waken'd by this tyranny
To ungod this child again, it could not be
  I should love her, who loves not me.

Rebel and atheist too, why murmur I,
  As though I felt the worst that love could do?
Love might make me leave loving, or might try
  A deeper plague, to make her love me too,
Which, since she loves before, I am loth to see;
Falsehood is worse than hate; and that must be,
  If she whom I love, should love me.

LOVE'S DEITY

3 *he who then lov'd most*] i.e. even the man who loved more than anyone else did.

5 *produc'd a destiny*] ordained a fate for lovers.

6 *vice-nature*] 'second nature': but probably there is also a derogatory play on the word 'vice'.

8 *meant not so much*] possibly: 'did not mean to give him so much power'; alternatively: 'did not mean it to have this effect'.

9 *in his young godhead*] i.e. during the early part of his period of godhead.

10 *even*] of the same degree.

11–12] His function was obligingly to pair off the passive lovers with their corresponding active lovers (i.e., presumably, the women with the men).

14] i.e. nothing was love unless it was mutual.

15 *will*] wants to.

17–18] i.e. all these actions fall within the scope of love.

26 *loves before*] has a lover already.

27 *that must be*] that is what it would necessarily be.

27–8] Cf. *Twickenham Garden*, ll. 26–7.

LOVE'S DIET

To what a cumbersome unwieldiness
And burdenous corpulence my love had grown,
    But that I did, to make it less,
    And keep it in proportion,
Give it a diet, made it feed upon
That which love worst endures, *discretion*.

Above one sigh a day I allow'd him not,
Of which my fortune, and my faults, had part;
    And if sometimes by stealth he got
    A she-sigh from my mistress' heart,
And thought to feast on that, I let him see
'Twas neither very sound, nor meant to me:

If he wrung from me a tear, I brin'd it so
With scorn or shame, that him it nourish'd not;
    If he suck'd hers, I let him know
    'Twas not a tear which he had got,
His drink was counterfeit, as was his meat;
For eyes which roll towards all, weep not, but sweat.

Whatever he would díctate, I writ that,
But burnt my letters; when she writ to me,
    And that that favour made him fat,
    I said: 'If any title be
Convey'd by this, ah! what doth it avail
To be the fortieth name in an entail?'

Thus I reclaim'd my buzzard love, to fly
At what, and when, and how, and where I choose;
    Now negligent of sport I lie,
    And now, as other falconers use,
I spring a mistress, swear, write, sigh and weep:
And the game kill'd, or lost, go talk, and sleep.

LOVE'S DIET

4 *proportion*] pronounced as four syllables.

6 *discretion*] pronounced as four syllables.

8] in which allowance, sighs for my ill-fortune and for my own faults had their share.

12 *sound*] sincere.

to] for.

12] Mr John Hayward (Nonesuch Donne, p. 765) points out two difficulties: (1) that if the sigh was not meant for Donne, it would not seem to matter whether it was 'sound' or not; (2) that 'meant to me' in the sense of 'meant for me', is not quoted in *O.E.D.* This made Mr Hayward incline to adopt Mr John Sparrow's suggested emendation: ' 'Twas neither very sound nor meat to me'. He did not, however, print the emendation. With respect, I do not think point (1) very strong against the old reading. It seems quite sensible to say: 'The sigh was not very sound, and, in any case, it was not meant for me.' Mr Hayward's second point seems stronger, and he supports it by saying that even if *O.E.D.* had overlooked the use, it seems odd that Donne should have used it in preference to the more common 'meant for'. Mr Sparrow's emendation seems distinctly possible. Stanza 2 clearly deals with the 'meat' which the poet's love feasts on, while stanza 3 deals with the drink. (L. 17 clearly refers back to the sighs of stanza 2.) On the other hand, this is not conclusive in favour of the emendation; since stanza 2 would still be referring to the meat for Donne's love, even if it did not mention the meat by name. In view of the lack of textual support from the MSS and old editions, therefore, I have decided to resist a strong temptation to print Mr Sparrow's emendation.

It is perhaps worth mention that *Lut* reads 'ment to bee'.

13 *brin'd*] salted.

17 *meat*] i.e. the sighs referred to in the preceding stanza.

21] We should, in modern English, of course, simply say: 'And that favour made him fat'.

24] The fortieth person named as a remainderman in an entail would have a very slender chance of coming into possession.

25 *buzzard*] a rapacious but sluggish species of hawk. Here the word has possibly also the secondary sense of 'blockhead' or 'dunce'. (Dr Johnson quotes a passage from Ascham in which it is used in that sense.)

27, 28 *Now . . . now*] sometimes . . . sometimes . . .

29 *spring*] start or rouse (the correct hawking term).

swear, write, sigh and weep] the love-falconer's methods of killing his game.

30 *go talk, and sleep*] So most MSS, and the 1633 edition, followed by Grierson. The 1635–69 editions and some MSS read 'go talk, or sleep'. The point may not be one of much importance, but the former reading appears to me slightly superior as suggesting a definite routine.

THE WILL

Before I sigh my last gasp, let me breathe,
Great Love, some legacies: Here I bequeath
Mine eyes to Argus, if mine eyes can see,
If they be blind, then, Love, I give them thee;
My tongue to Fame; to ambassadors mine ears;
To women or the sea, my tears:
Thou, Love, hast taught me heretofore
By making me serve her who had twenty more,
That I should give to none but such as had too much before.

My constancy I to the planets give;
My truth to them who at the Court do live;
Mine ingenuity and openness,
To Jesuits; to buffoons my pensiveness;
My silence to any who abroad hath been;
My money to a Capuchin:
Thou, Love, taught'st me, by appointing me
To love there, where no love receiv'd can be,
Only to give to such as have an incapacity.

My faith I give to Roman Catholics;
All my good works unto the Schismatics
Of Amsterdam; my best civility
And courtship, to an University;
My modesty I give to soldiers bare;
My patience let gamesters share:
Thou, Love, taught'st me, by making me
Love her that holds my love disparity,
Only to give to those that count my gifts indignity.

THE WILL

3 *Argus*] The Greek mythological character who was appointed by Hera to guard Io after her metamorphosis into a heifer. Argus had a hundred eyes, and was therefore surnamed 'Panoptes' (the all-seeing). (See Smith's Classical Dictionary.)
5 *ambassadors*] possibly a hit at the spying activities of some contemporary ambassador or ambassadors in London.

12 *ingenuity*] ingenuousness, freedom from dissimulation.
15] probably a quip at the abuse of begging by the Friars, who were, of course, vowed to poverty. It seems similar in form to La Fontaine's stroke (at the end of the fable *Le Rat qui s'est retiré du Monde*):

Un moine ? Non, mais un dervis:
Je suppose qu'un moine est toujours charitable.

Donne, I suggest, is ironically affecting to believe in the sincerity of the Friars' vows, just as La Fontaine is pretending to believe in the charity of monks.
18 *have an incapacity*] i.e. are unable to make use of the gifts.
19] If this is, as seems possible, an attack on the Jesuit doctrine that faith alone is insufficient for salvation without co-operant good works, then it is a very poor one, since the Jesuits did not deny the efficacy of faith, and even maintained, like all orthodox Catholics, its necessity for salvation.
19 *Cathòlics*] It is essential to pronounce the word as a trisyllable here.
20] This shot at the extreme Puritan Schismatics of Amsterdam, who believed in justification by faith alone, is more effective, since they considered good works entirely inefficacious for salvation.
21–2 *my best civility . . . University*] seemingly an attack on the boorishness of some of the contemporary dons.
24 *patience*] trisyllabic.
26 *disparity*] i.e. beneath her.

I give my reputation to those
Which were my friends; mine industry to foes;
To Schoolmen I bequeath my doubtfulness;
My sickness to physicians, or excess;
To Nature, all that I in rhyme have writ;
And to my company my wit:
Thou, Love, by making me adore
Her, who begot this love in me before,
Taught'st me to make as though I gave, when I do but restore.

To him for whom the passing bell next tolls,
I give my physic books; my written rolls
Of moral counsels, I to Bedlam give;
My brazen medals, unto them which live
In want of bread; to them which pass among
All foreigners, mine English tongue:
Thou, Love, by making me love one
Who thinks her friendship a fit portion
For younger lovers, dost my gifts thus disproportion.

Therefore I'll give no more; but I'll undo
The world by dying; because love dies too.
Then all your beauties will be no more worth
Than gold in mines, where none doth draw it forth;
And all your graces no more use shall have
Than a sun-dial in a grave:
Thou, Love, taught'st me, by making me
Love her, who doth neglect both me and thee,
To invent, and practise, this one way to annihilate all three.

28 *reputation*] '-ation' trisyllabic.

29 *mine industry to foes*] probably because hard work is often the result of attacks or unscrupulous rivalry by enemies.

36 *do*] The general tenor of the poem seems to warrant this adoption of the reading of the 1635–69 editions and of one MS, in preference to the reading 'did', which appears in the 1633 edition, and in the other MSS consulted by Grierson. Donne is *now* restoring, by his will.

44 *portion*] trisyllabic.

45 *disproportion*] '-portion' trisyllabic.

THE FUNERAL

Whoever comes to shroud me, do not harm
        Nor question much
That subtle wreath of hair, which crowns my arm;
The mystery, the sign, you must not touch,
        For 'tis my outward Soul,
Viceroy to that, which then to heaven being gone,
        Will leave this to control,
And keep these limbs, her provinces, from dissolution.

For if the sinewy thread my brain lets fall
        Through every part,
Can tie those parts, and make me one of all;
These hairs which upward grew, and strength and art
        Have from a better brain,
Can better do it; except she meant that I
        By this should know my pain,
As prisoners then are manacled, when they're condemn'd to die.

Whate'er she meant by it, bury it with me,
        For since I am
Love's martyr, it might breed idolatry,
If into others' hands these relics came;
        As 'twas humility
To afford to it all that a soul can do,
        So, 'tis some bravery,
That since you would save none of me, I bury some of you.

THE FUNERAL

2 *question much*] ask much about.

3] cf. *The Relic*, l. 6.

8 *dissolution*] to be pronounced as five syllables.

9 *the sinewy thread my brain lets fall*] probably the filaments of the nervous system. In a sermon Donne speaks of 'A Brain which shall send forth sinews and ligaments, to tye sins together.' I think it is more than probable that in that passage also Donne was using the term to denote the nerve tracts. The term 'sinew' was certainly often used in his time to mean 'nerve' (last use recorded by *O.E.D.*, 1621). The word is clearly used in this sense in the following passage from Sir John Davies describing the sensory nervous system:

> The feeling pow'r, which is life's root,
> Through ev'ry living part itself doth shed
> By sinews, which extend from head to foot;
> And, like a net, all o'er the body spread.

11 *and make me one of all*] and co-ordinate all parts into the single being which is myself.

14 *except*] unless perhaps . . .

19 *idolatry*] cf. *The Relic*, stanza 2.

22 *To afford to it all that a soul can do*] A difficult line, probably meaning: 'to confer on it all that a Soul can confer', viz. its viceroyalty: alternatively, 'to credit it with all the powers of a soul.' (Cf. in either case, stanza 1.)

23] i.e. so, by way of compensation, it is a touch of bravado.

THE BLOSSOM

Little think'st thou, poor flower,
Whom I have watch'd six or seven days,
And seen thy birth, and seen what every hour
Gave to thy growth, thee to this height to raise,
And now dost laugh and triumph on this bough,
Little think'st thou
That it will freeze anon, and that I shall
Tomorrow find thee fall'n, or not at all.

Little think'st thou, poor heart,
That labour'st yet to nestle thee,
And think'st by hovering here to get a part
In a forbidden or forbidding tree,
And hop'st her stiffness by long siege to bow,
Little think'st thou
That thou tomorrow, ere that Sun doth wake,
Must with this sun and me a journey take.

But thou which lov'st to be
Subtle to plague thyself, wilt say:
'Alas! if you must go, what's that to me?
Here lies my business, and here I will stay:
You go to friends, whose love and means present
Various content
To your eyes, ears, and tongue, and every part.
If then your body go, what need you a heart?'

Well then, stay here; but know,
When thou hast stay'd and done thy most,
A naked thinking heart, that makes no show,
Is, to a woman, but a kind of ghost;
How shall she know my heart; or, having none,
Know thee for one?
Practice may make her know some other part;
But take my word, she doth not know a heart.

Meet me at London, then,
Twenty days hence, and thou shalt see
Me fresher, and more fat, by being with men,
Than if I had stay'd still with her and thee.
For God's sake, if you can, be you so too:
I would give you
There, to another friend, whom we shall find
As glad to have my body, as my mind.

THE BLOSSOM

9 *heart*] Throughout the poem there is play on 'heart' as (1) the soul or mind, as seat of the affections and will, and (2) the physical heart.
12 *forbidden or forbidding*] 'forbidden' suggesting that the relationship Donne desires is illicit; 'forbidding' implying that the woman is trying to repel his advances towards a physical relationship.
15 *that Sun*] i.e. his lady; cf. *A Nocturnal upon St Lucy's Day*, ll. 37–9.
16 *this sun*] i.e. the ordinary sun.
17–18] 'But you, who love to refine on your self-torture, . . .'
22 *content*] satisfaction.
26 *done thy most*] i.e. to please his mistress.
27 *A naked thinking heart*] probably meaning a heart which merely feels about its mistress, without being able to show her attentions (because of the absence of the rest of the body or of the body as a whole).

THE PRIMROSE

Upon this primrose hill
Where, if Heav'n would distil
A shower of rain, each several drop might go
To his own primrose, and grow manna so;
And where their form, and their infinity
Make a terrestrial galaxy,
As the small stars do in the sky:
I walk to find a true love; and I see
That 'tis not a mere woman that is she,
But must or more or less than woman be.

Yet know I not, which flower
I wish; a six, or four;
For should my true-love less than woman be,
She were scarce anything; and then, should she
Be more than woman, she would get above
All thought of sex, and think to move
My heart to study her, and not to love;
Both these were monsters; since there must reside
Falsehood in woman, I could more abide
She were by art, than Nature, falsified.

Live, Primrose, then, and thrive
With thy true number, five;
And woman, whom this flower doth represent,
With this mysterious number be content;
Ten is the farthest number; if half ten
Belong unto each woman, then
Each woman may take half us men;
Or, if this will not serve their turn, since all
Numbers are odd, or even, and they fall
First into this five, women may take us all.

THE PRIMROSE

Note on the title: The sub-title (given for the first time in the 1635 edition) is 'being at Montgomery Castle, upon the hill, on which it is situate.' At the time when the poem was probably written, it may be that it was no longer the home of Magdalen Herbert, but it still belonged to her family.

2–4 *Where . . . grow manna so*] i.e. where there are so many primroses that if Heaven should let fall a shower of rain upon it, each single drop would be able to find its home in a primrose, and so turn into vital food. (I owe this interpretation to discussion with Professor Grierson.)

6 *galaxy*] Milky Way.

5–7] Professor Coffin has pointed out that these lines make it almost certain the poem was written after the publication of Galileo's *Siderius Nuncius* (1610), where telescopic evidence for the view that the Galaxy consisted of an immense number of small stars was first announced. There is support elsewhere for the view that Donne knew Galileo's discovery. As Professor Coffin also indicates, however, this *theory* of the Galaxy had been held by various writers since ancient times. (See C. M. Coffin, *John Donne and the New Philosophy*, Columbia U.P., New York, 1937.)

8 *a true love*] playing on the two senses (1) a beloved, (2) a primrose with an irregular number of petals (i.e. more or less than five), considered as a symbol of faithful love (see note on l. 12 below). I think Grierson does not represent the precise situation when he says (op. cit., II. 48) that Donne is seeking for a primrose to symbolize his love, but 'fears to find either more or less'. Donne is not at first looking for a five-petalled primrose, he is looking for a six or four, since those oddities were considered symbols of faithful love. He only renounces sixes and fours later, when he has seen what creature would correspond to them.

12 *a six, or four*] a six-petalled, or four-petalled primrose. With regard to the six-petalled primrose, Chambers quotes from Browne's *Britannia's Pastorals* a passage in which such a primrose is described as being used as a 'true-love', i.e. as a symbol of faithful love. A four-leafed *clover* is still regarded as auspicious to lovers.

19–20 *I could . . . falsified*] i.e., 'I would far rather have her made false artificially, than that she should be false by nature.' 'Art' possibly corresponds to deliberate interference, such as seduction. It is just conceivable that Donne is here casting a wistful glance at the possibility that he might be the seducer.

25 *Ten is the farthest number*] i.e. the number at the upper extreme of the scale 1–10.

25–7] i.e. if ten be taken to correspond to the whole of each man, and each woman counts for five, then each woman can have half of each man.

28–30] 'Or, if they are not satisfied with that, then, since all numbers are odd or even' (and therefore any number or numbers chosen to represent a man are either odd or even), 'and since the numbers which symbolize or represent the odd and even' (2 and 3, 1 not counting) 'are

[*continued on p. 109*]

THE RELIC

When my grave is broke up again
Some second guest to entertain
(For graves have learn'd that woman-head,
To be to more than one a bed),
And he that digs it spies
A bracelet of bright hair about the bone,
Will he not let us alone,
And think that there a loving couple lies,
Who thought that this device might be some way
To make their souls, at the last busy day,
Meet at this grave, and make a little stay?

If this fall in a time, or land,
Where mis-devotion doth command,
Then he that digs us up will bring
Us to the Bishop, and the King,
To make us relics; then
Thou shalt be a Mary Magdalen, and I
A something else thereby;
All women shall adore us, and some men;
And, since at such time miracles are sought,
I would have that age by this paper taught
What miracles we harmless lovers wrought.

First, we lov'd well and faithfully,
Yet knew not what we lov'd, nor why;
Difference of sex we never knew,
No more than our guardian angels do;
Coming and going, we
Perchance might kiss, but not between those meals;
Our hands ne'er touch'd the seals
Which nature, injur'd by late law, sets free:
These miracles we did; but now, alas,
All measure, and all language, I should pass,
Should I tell what a miracle she was.

THE RELIC

1–2] Common by Donne's time where burial-ground was crowded.

3 *woman-head*] 'womanly nature', with a possible undertone derived from the similarity of form to 'maidenhead'.

6] cf. *The Funeral*, l. 3.

9 *thought*] Some MSS I have seen, e.g. *A25*, *C57* and *Lut*, give an interesting alternative reading: 'hop'd'.

10 *last busy day*] the Resurrection.

12 *this*] i.e. the digging-up of my body. *fall*] happen.

13 *mis-devotion*] 'false idolatry'. In view of what follows it is probable that Donne is here covertly attacking Roman Catholicism. The use of relics had been abandoned in all the Reformed churches.

15 *the Bishop, and the King*] This is a somewhat strange phrase; if the reference is meant to be to Roman Catholic practice, it appears to be, technically at least, mistaken. The King never had any power in the Roman Church discipline to recognize relics, i.e. to recognize any physical object as a relic. Kings, on the other hand, had from time to time assisted in the translation of relics, i.e. their transference to a shrine where they could be venerated. Edward I, for example, assisted in the translation of the remains of St Hugh of Lincoln. Bishops, however, from early Christian times, had recognized relics, and this practice was specifically enjoined by the Council of Trent at about the middle of the sixteenth century. (For further details see the Catholic Encyclopaedia, Articles *Relics, Beatification and Canonization.*) On the other hand, a Council of Metz in 813 required that the sanction of either the prince or the bishop, and the permission of a sacred synod should be obtained for the *translation* of relics (see the Encyclopaedia of Religion and Ethics).

18 *A something else*] This phrase is capable of two interpretations. It may mean simply (1) 'some other relic', or it may (2) have a very bold sense, namely, that people in that age of 'misdevotion' will take Donne's bone for one of Christ's. Mr R. C. Cook, of Christ's College, with whom I have discussed this line, has rightly suggested to me that

---

THE PRIMROSE [*continued*

contained in this number five' (since they add up to it), 'then women may each take all of a man.' (I owe much to Grierson's note here, though my interpretation as a whole differs from his.)

30 *this five*] Grierson finds difficulty here, and punctuates 'this, five', taking the two words as in apposition; but the phrase 'this five' seems to me more satisfactory as it stands. It seems to represent just that play of almost childish fancy, in which Donne is indulging in much of this poem. Children playing dominoes often say such things as 'there's that double six again' or 'I don't like this double five'. The demonstrative adjective expresses a sort of intimacy, and the usage is perhaps a case of incipient animism.

the very possibility of interpretation (1) is itself some support to interpretation (2), since it would afford a cover against any imputation of blasphemy. In any case, as Mr Cook has also urged, Donne is only attributing such a thought to an age of 'mis-devotion'. Interpretation (2) is a teasing possibility, and I am inclined to think it is the right one, since interpretation (1) is so tame. Mr F. L. Lucas tells me that he had independently hit upon the idea of Christ as the only possible one. He has suggested to me that support for it could be found in Luther's pronouncement that Christ and the Magdalen were lovers.

thereby] i.e. through the action of the Bishop and the King. (I owe this point to Mr J. Russell, of Trinity Hall.)

19 *adore*] Again, it may be worth pointing out that in strict Roman Catholic practice relics are not adored but venerated. No doubt, though, actual practice has often enough deviated from pure doctrine.

and some men] possibly a cynical distinction, constituting a hit at the credulity of women: or possibly, simply, as Mr F. L. Lucas has suggested to me, a reference to the greater interest of women in love romances.

20] That God 'fittingly honours relics by working miracles in their presence' is categorically stated by St Thomas Aquinas (*Summa Theol.*, III. 9. 25. 6). They came to be particularly expected at the time of consecration.

21 *this paper*] i.e. the poem.

24 *what*] i.e. what in each other.

25–6] After considerable hesitation I have decided to adopt the reading of the Bridgewater MS and the British Museum Stowe MS 961, instead of the reading of the 1633 edition and of a few MSS, which was adopted by Grierson. That reading was:

Difference of sex no more we knew,
Than our guardian angels do, . . .

(Grierson has a semi-colon here.) The majority of the MSS, including some of the highest authority, read:

Difference of sex we never knew,
More than our guardian angels do.

This reading seems to me preferable to that adopted by Grierson. The line: 'Than our guardian angels do, . . .' has always seemed to me very weak. On the other hand, the reading: 'More than our guardian angels do' has its own disadvantage, namely that the word 'more' cannot bear the weight of the antecedent clause. 'Any more' or 'no more' seems to be required. There is no authority for 'Any more', but there is the MS authority I have mentioned, for the reading I have adopted. This reading also receives some support from the fact that all the remaining printed editions 1635–1719 read:

Difference of sex we never knew,
No more than guardian angels do.

All the MSS, however, according to Grierson, contain the word 'our', and, on that ground, the reading adopted seems preferable to that of the printed editions 1635–1719. I suspected their omission of the word 'our' of being merely an editorial attempt to make the metre quite regular, until I found that this is also the reading of *Lut*.

27 *Coming and going*] Grierson points out that this was one of the uses of kissing sanctioned in the Bible. He also points out that Erasmus, writing in 1499, seems to regard the kiss of salutation and the kiss of parting as specially English.

28 *meals*] the kiss being the food of the soul.

29–30 *Our hands . . . free*] 'We never attempted that physical union which Nature allows to all, but which upstart human laws have subjected to restraint.' The passage is, as Grierson has pointed out to me, a close imitation of Ovid, *Metamorphoses*, x. 329 ff. (cf. also Grierson, *Criticism and Creation*, 1950, p. 104). The lines in Ovid are as follows:

Felices quibus ista licent! Humana malignas
Cura dedit leges et quod natura remittit
Invida jura negant.

These lines are rendered by Golding, the Elizabethan translator, as follows:

In happy case they are
That may do so without offence; but man's malicious care
Hath made a bridle for itself, and spiteful laws restrain
The things that nature setteth free . . .

Myrrha is defending to herself her unlawful passion for her own father, and in these lines she is envying the animals, who are not bound by human laws against incest. The verbal similarity of Donne's l. 30 to the last clause in the passage from Golding is striking. There are other passages in Donne's own work which are closely parallel, e.g. ll. 191–203 of *The Progresse of the Soule*. The last three lines of that passage are as follows:

Men, till they took laws which made freedom less,
Their daughters, and their sisters did ingress;
Till now unlawful, therefore ill, 'twas not.

31 *but now, alas*] possibly either (1) a cry of grief as he is called back to the present, when, as the poem runs, his lady has long been dead; or (2) an apology that he could not restrain the praises of his lady within the limitations even of language. Both elements may be present.

32–3] 'I should exceed all bounds and even the resources of language itself, were I to say what a miracle she herself was!'

THE DAMP

When I am dead, and doctors know not why,
And my friends' curiosity
Will have me cut up to survey each part,
When they shall find your picture in my heart,
You think a sudden damp of love
Will through all their senses move,
And work on them as me, and so prefer
Your murder, to the name of massacre.

Poor victories; but if you dare be brave,
And pleasure in your conquest have,
First kill the enormous giant, your *Disdain*,
And let the enchantress *Honqur* next be slain,
And like a Goth and Vandal rise,
Deface recórds, and histories
Of your own arts and triumphs over men,
And without such advantage kill me then.

For I could muster up as well as you
My giants, and my witches too,
Which are vast *Constancy*, and *Secretness*,
But these I neither look for, nor profess;
Kill me as woman, let me die
As a mere man; do you but try
Your passive valour, and you shall find then,
Naked you've odds enough of any man.

THE DAMP

Title and 5 *damp*] 'chill depression', a metaphor taken from cold foggy night air.

7 *prefer*] promote.

20 *neither look for, nor profess*] i.e. neither look for in you nor profess in myself.

21–4] an ingenious transition to a clear invitation to sexuality.

23 *then*] One of the awkward cases in modernization of the spelling. The reading of the old editions and MSS is 'than' (meaning 'then'). I have, however, felt bound to print 'then' since 'than' in this sense is not a modern word: but I have felt equally bound to point out that the faulty rhyme which results is not Donne's.

24 *Naked*] I have ventured to adopt the bolder reading of the 1635–69 editions and of most of the MSS, including some of high authority, in preference to the less vivid reading 'In that' of the 1633 edition and of a few of the MSS, which was adopted by Grierson.

THE DISSOLUTION

She's dead; and all which die
To their first elements resolve;
And we were mutual elements to us,
And made of one another.
My body then doth hers involve,
And those things whereof I consist, hereby
In me abundant grow, and burdenous,
And nourish not, but smother.
My fire of passion, sighs of air,
Water of tears, and earthly sad despair,
Which my materials be,
(But near worn out by love's security),
She, to my loss, doth by her death repair;
And I might live long wretched so,
But that my fire doth with my fuel grow.
Now, as those active kings
Whose foreign conquest treasure brings,
Receive more, and spend more, and soonest break:
This—which I am amaz'd that I can speak—
This death, hath with my store
My use increas'd.
And so my soul, more earnestly releas'd,
Will outstrip hers; as bullets flown before
A latter bullet may o'ertake, the powder being more.

THE DISSOLUTION

5 *involve*] comprise, include.

6 *those things whereof I consist*] i.e. my elements.
hereby] i.e. by her death.

7] because of the sudden dumping of crude elements in my body after her dissolution.

8] because they are not organized, but in a crude state.

9–12] i.e. my four elements, which had almost ceased to exist in me in their crude state, because of the security I felt in reciprocated love.

10 *earthly*] (an old form): 'earthy'.

13 *repair*] here 'replenish'.

14 *wretched*] i.e. because smothered with crude elements.

15] 'if it were not for the fact that my element of fire is replenished at the same time as my fuel elements are.' (The element of fire (passion) is, of course, increased through being thwarted by the loss of his lady.)

18 *break*] become insolvent.

19 *speak*] speak of.

21 *use*] expenditure.

22 *earnestly*] 'ardently, eagerly'; because of his fire of passion consuming the rest of his body more rapidly than in the case of normal dissolution.

23 *flown*] i.e. shot into the air.

24 *the powder being more*] when the explosive charge is greater.

A JET RING SENT

Thou art not so black as my heart,
Nor half so brittle as her heart, thou art;
What wouldst thou say? Shall both our properties by thee be spoke,
Nothing more endless, nothing sooner broke?

Marriage rings are not of this stuff;
Oh, why should aught less precious or less tough
Figure our loves? except in thy name thou have bid it say:
'I'm cheap, and naught but fashion, fling me away.'

Yet stay with me since thou art come,
Circle this finger's top, which didst her thumb.
Be justly proud, and gladly safe, that thou dost dwell with me,
She that, oh, broke her faith, would soon break thee.

A JET RING SENT

3 *spoke*] i.e. symbolized.

6 *less precious or less tough*] i.e. than gold.

7 *Figure*] represent.

8 *fling me away*] almost certainly a pun on 'jet' and French 'jette' (throw away), as Mr F. L. Lucas suggested to Mr John Hayward (see Nonesuch Donne, p. 766).

10 *her thumb*] Chambers points out that thumb-rings were commonly worn by prosperous citizens, and quotes *1 Hen. IV*, II. iv. 364; and this passage suggests that women also wore them.

NEGATIVE LOVE
or
THE NOTHING

I never stoop'd so low, as they
Which on an eye, cheek, lip, can prey;
  Seldom to them, which soar no higher
  Than virtue or the mind to admire:
For sense, and understanding, may
  Know what gives fuel to their fire.
My love, though silly, is more brave,
For may I miss, whene'er I crave,
If I know yet, what I would have.

If that be simply perfectest
Which can by no way be express'd
  But *negatives*, my love is so.
  To All, which all love, I say no.
If any who deciphers best
  What we know not, our selves, can know,
Let him teach me that nothing; this
As yet my ease and comfort is:
Though I speed not, I cannot miss.

NEGATIVE LOVE or THE NOTHING

Note on the title: Negative Love is the title given in the 1633–69 editions and in most of the MSS. A few MSS give as title *The Nothing*. A few MSS give both titles. I have preserved both titles, as each title seems to me to make a distinct contribution to the understanding of the poem.

1–2 *they . . . prey*] completely physical lovers.

3 *Seldom*] note this distinction from the 'never' case of ll. 1–2.
to them] as far as those.

3–4 *them . . . admire*] 'Platonic' lovers.

7 *brave*] here probably used in the modern sense of 'courageous'.

8 *miss*] i.e. fail to obtain what I want.
whene'er I crave] whenever I want a woman.

8–9] cf. *A Valediction: forbidding mourning*, ll. 17–18, and *The Ecstasy*, ll. 29–32.

13] A not altogether easy line. It probably means: 'I decline all the positive perfections, which are what everybody loves'.

15 *What we know not, our selves*] Professor Grierson (op. cit. II. 50) quotes pertinently from Donne's Sermons a passage in which Donne suggests that the reason why Adam did not name himself when he named creatures, was that he knew himself least.

14–16] If any subtle psychologist, able to read our enigmatic hearts for us, *can* find out the answer, let him tell me what that nothing is which I want.

17 *As yet*] in the meanwhile.

18] 'Though I make no progress, I cannot fail to obtain what I want' (because he wants nothing).

THE PROHIBITION

Take heed of loving me;
At least remember, I forbade it thee:
Not that I shall repair my unthrifty waste
Of breath and blood, upon thy sighs and tears,
By being to thee then what to me thou wast;
But so great joy our life at once outwears:
Then, lest thy love, by my death, frustrate be,
If thou love me, take heed of loving me.

Take heed of hating me,
Or too much triumph in the victory:
Not that I shall be mine own officer,
And hate with hate again retaliate;
But thou wilt lose the style of conqueror,
If I, thy conquest, perish by thy hate:
Then, lest my being nothing lessen thee,
If thou hate me, take heed of hating me.

Yet, love and hate me too;
So, these extremes shall neither's office do:
Love me, that I may die the gentler way;
Hate me, because thy love's too great for me;
Or let these two, themselves, not me, decay;
So shall I, live, thy stage, not triumph, be:
Then, lest thy love, hate, and me thou undo,
Oh, let me live, yet love and hate me too.

THE PROHIBITION

General Note: In the Bridgewater manuscript the first two stanzas of this poem are headed *J.D.* and the last *T.R.* In Group II manuscripts (see Introduction, p. xlvi) the third stanza is omitted. This suggests that the third stanza was either written or at least suggested by one of Donne's friends, possibly Sir Thomas Roe. However large a part his friend may have played in creating the excellent third stanza, however, it is certainly of a piece with Donne's own work.

1 *Take heed of*] beware of.

4 *upon*] from, i.e. by drawing upon.

5 *what to me thou wast*] viz. cold.

6 *joy*] i.e. the joy of mutual love.

10 *victory*] i.e. the victory of having captured him without having lost her own heart.

11 *mine own officer*] not very clear, I think: possibly meaning that he will not, like an officer of the law, simply mete out justice, i.e. repay hatred with hatred: or possibly, simply 'not that I shall take my own part', as a representative (officer) takes the part of the person or power he represents.

15 *lessen thee*] diminish your glory.

18] 'In that way, these extremes of love and hate will not perform their respective functions' (*not* 'each other's functions').

19 *the gentler way*] i.e. through excess of joy in your love.

19–20] i.e. he asks her to love him so that he shall not die in the way described in stanza 2: and to hate him so that he shall not die in the way described in stanza 1.

21 *decay*] here used transitively.

22 *live*] still alive.

stage] I follow Grierson here in adopting the reading of the 1635–69 editions and of the majority of the MSS, in preference to 'staye', the reading of the 1633 edition. Grierson's note is, however, misleading. He says: 'All the MSS I have consulted support "stage"': but in his text he quotes two MSS of very high authority as reading 'staye' and one MS of less authority as reading 'stay'. 'Stay' (or 'staye'), therefore, has considerable authority. It also makes good sense, even though it is rather tame. Nevertheless, I think Grierson is right in saying that 'stage' gives the best meaning, namely, to quote his explanation: 'Alive, I shall continue to be the stage on which your victories are daily set forth; dead, I shall be but your triumph, a thing achieved once, never to be repeated.'

23–4] Here, as in so many other places, we owe a debt to Grierson, for clearing up textual confusion. I cannot quite agree with him, however, if he implies (II, p. 51) that there are only two versions of these lines which can be valid, viz. (1) the 1633 reading

Lest thou thy love and hate and me undo
To let me live, Oh love and hate me too.

which Grierson himself adopts; and (2) what he calls 'the version of the MSS':

Then lest thy love, hate, and me thou undo,
O let me live, O love and hate me too.

'Yet' for 'O', in the middle of the last line, has also MS authority. This version seems to me to be better writing and more characteristic of Donne than the version containing the rather monotonous repetition of 'Oh' or 'O' in the last line. The force of 'yet' seems to me as follows: If she is to preserve all three things (1) her love, (2) her hate, (3) Donne, she must preserve *him* ('Oh, let me live' thus corresponds to, and ties up, the first two stanzas); but the first two stanzas suggest that she cannot do this if she hates or loves him. The third stanza, however, shows how she can preserve him, and *yet* love and hate him too. Another advantage of the reading I have adopted is that, unlike the 1633 reading adopted by Grierson, it preserves the pattern set by the penultimate lines of the first two stanzas, since each of those lines begins with the word 'Then'.

23] Mr F. L. Lucas has suggested to me that it is perhaps worth pointing out that if my suggested text of ll. 23–4 be adopted, both metre and logic demand that the word 'and' before 'me' should be stressed in reading.

THE EXPIRATION
(A Valediction)

So, so, break off this last lamenting kiss,
  Which sucks two souls, and vapours both away;
Turn thou, ghost, that way, and let me turn this,
  And let ourselves benight our happiest day:
We ask'd none leave to love; nor will we owe
  Any so cheap a death, as saying: 'Go':

Go; and if that word have not quite kill'd thee,
  Ease me with death, by bidding me go too:
Or, if it have, let my word work on me,
  And a just office on a murderer do.
Except it be too late to kill me so,
  Being double dead, going, and bidding go.

THE EXPIRATION

Note on the title: The title in the printed editions 1633–69 is *The Expiration.* In some MSS the title is *An Expiration.* Other MSS give *Valediction, Valedictio Amoris* and *Valedico.* To make clear the character of the poem I have introduced the idea given by these MSS as a sub-title.

2 *vapours*] evaporates.

5–6] We didn't ask anyone for permission to love each other when our love began; and we will not give anyone the easy task of killing us by telling us to part.

9 *Or*] This is the reading of the printed editions 1635–69, and of some of the MSS. The 1633 edition and other MSS read 'Oh'. There is not much to choose between the readings. 'Oh' is more emotional, 'Or' more logical. In this case I think the more logical reading slightly preferable.

11 *Except*] unless.

11–12] Unless it is too late to kill me in this way, since I am already doubly dead, through leaving you and through telling you to leave me.

THE COMPUTATION

For the first twenty years, since yesterday,
  I scarce believ'd thou couldst be gone away;
For forty more, I fed on favours past,
  And forty on hopes, that thou wouldst they might last;
Tears drown'd one hundred, and sighs blew out two;
  A thousand, I did neither think, nor do,
  Or not divide, all being one thought of you;
  Or, in a thousand more, forgot that too.
Yet call not this long life; but think that I
Am, by being dead, immortal; can ghosts die?

THE COMPUTATION

1] Another allusion to the length of 'Lovers' hours' (cf. *The Legacy*, ll. 3–4).

4] *that . . . last*] 'that you might be willing for the favours to continue'.

6–7] 'For a thousand years I neither thought of anything nor did anything, or else it was that I didn't distinguish one thought or act from another, because all my activity consisted in thinking a single thought, the thought of you.'

8] A difficult line. Possibly it takes up the two previous lines, and continues: 'Or perhaps what happened was that in another thousand years I even forgot about that thought of you.' Alternatively it may mean: 'Or perhaps in the next thousand years I forgot what happened in the previous thousand years (being so concentrated on thinking about you).'

9–10] The sense is: 'Don't call this long life, though; think of me rather as having died (through being absent from you), and therefore become immortal. It was only by being incapable of dying again, because I was already a departed spirit, that I was able to subsist for that length of time.'

THE PARADOX

No lover saith: 'I love', nor any other
    Can judge a perfect lover;
He thinks that else none can, nor will agree
    That any loves but he:
I cannot say I lov'd, for who can say
    He was kill'd yesterday?
Love with excess of heat, more young, than old,
    Death kills with too much cold;
We die but once, and who lov'd last did die,
    He that saith twice, doth lie:
For though he seem to move, and stir a while,
    It doth the sense beguile.
Such life is like the light which bideth yet
    When the light's life is set,
Or like the heat, which fire in solid matter
    Leaves behind, two hours after.
Once I lov'd and died; and am now become
    Mine epitaph and tomb.
Here dead men speak their last, and so do I:
    Love-slain, lo! here I lie.

THE PARADOX

1 *No lover saith: 'I love'*] possibly because as soon as he loves he is at once struck dead (see below), or possibly because no true lover will reveal his love to others (the idea might be a relic of the code of courtly love).

any other] anyone but the lover himself.

3–4] 'The man who is completely in love thinks that nobody else *can* love but himself, and he will not agree that any one else *is in fact* in love.' Alternatively: 'The man who is completely in love thinks that nobody else can judge his love, and he will not agree that anyone else is in love either.' Of these interpretations I slightly prefer the second.

5–6] Nor can I say that I did love (using the past tense), for a man who was killed yesterday does not live to tell the tale.

1–6] The paradoxical situation therefore is that it is impossible for love to be attributed to anyone either (1) by himself (*a*) in the present tense, or (*b*) in the past tense; or (2) by anyone else. The 'solution' of the paradox, which is itself another paradox, comes in ll. 17–20.

7 *Love with . . . heat*] i.e. Love kills by excess of heat.

7–8] Mr F. L. Lucas has suggested to me what seems the most likely interpretation of these lines, namely: 'Love kills more of the young with too much heat than Death kills of the old with too much cold.' In the belief that this is the correct account of the sense, I have supplied a comma after 'young'.

9 *who lov'd last did die*] slightly obscure; it probably means: 'even the very last person who has been in love, has already died.'

10] Whoever says that he died twice, first through love, and then through death, is simply lying.

12] It is merely an illusion that he is still alive.

13–14] 'This sort of life is like the light that lingers on after sunset' ('The light's life', being, as Grierson says, the sun).

17–20] 'The only thing that I can say' (as a 'solution' of the paradox) 'is that I loved at one time' (probably playing on this meaning and the meaning 'once only'), 'and died, and have now become my own epitaph and tomb'.

19 *Here*] i.e. in the epitaphs on their tombs.

FAREWELL TO LOVE

Whilst yet to prove,
I thought there was some deity in love,
So did I reverence, and gave
Worship; as atheists at their dying hour
Call (what they cannot name) an unknown power,
As ignorantly did I crave:
Thus when
Things not yet known are coveted by men,
Our desires give them fashion, and so
As they wax lesser, fall, as they size, grow.

But, from late fair
His Highness (sitting in a golden chair)
Is not less cared for after three days
By children, than the thing which lovers so
Blindly admire, and with such worship woo;
Being had, enjoying it decays:
And thence,
What before pleas'd them all, takes but one sense,
And that so lamely, as it leaves behind
A kind of sorrowing dullness to the mind.

Ah, cannot we,
As well as cocks and lions, jocund be
After such pleasures? Unless wise
Nature decreed (since each such act, they say,
Diminisheth the length of life a day)
This, as she would man should despise
The sport,
Because that other curse of being short,
And only for a minute made to be,
Eagers desire, to raise posterity?

FAREWELL TO LOVE

1 *Whilst yet to prove*] While I had still no experience of love.

2–4 *I . . . Worship*] I thought that there was something divine in love, *and therefore* I reverenced and worshipped it.

5 *Call*] call upon.

6] so ignorant were my longings.

9 *fashion*] Either (1) worth, value, or, more probably, I think, (2) form, shape (see note on 9–10, below). (The word is here trisyllabic.)

9–10 *and . . . grow*] Somewhat obscure. Grammatically 'they', in each case, should refer to 'things not yet known'; but the resulting sense is not entirely satisfactory, since there is clearly no method of gauging the size of the 'things' other than by the size of the 'desires'. On the other hand, to take 'they' to refer to 'desires' makes the passage not merely tortuous, which would be typical enough of Donne, but also untidy, and untidiness is highly uncharacteristic of him. I think, therefore, that of these two the former interpretation is preferable. Yet neither is satisfactory, and it has therefore occurred to me that the sense is possibly more complex, namely, (starting at l. 7): 'thus when we wish for things as yet unknown to us, our desires give them a form, and then in turn dwindle or increase as that form grows less or bulks larger.'

10 *wax lesser*] grow less. *fall*] abate.

size] 'get larger, swell'. This ('sise') is the reading of the 1635–69 editions and of the MS O'F. The poem does not appear in the 1633 edition. A variant occurs in *S96*, viz. 'rise'. Palaeographically, 'r' and 's' are easily confused. If the reading 'rise' were adopted there would be a chiasmus, 'grow' then being opposed to 'wax lesser' and 'rise' to 'fall'. With the present reading 'grow' is opposed to 'fall' and 'size' to 'wax lesser'.

11-15] The sense may be: 'But lovers, after three days, no more bother about the act of love which they wonder at so blindly, and court with so much worship, than children do about some prince sitting on a gilt throne, which has been bought for them at a recent fair.' (Chambers thought the prince was probably made of gingerbread. As Professor Legouis points out, however, the children would, in that case, probably have eaten him. I had thought this point could be circumvented by supposing that the children only *saw* the prince, but 'from' does suggest that they have come to possess him.)

16] Once the experience has taken place, the enjoyment of it peters out.

18 *them all*] all the senses.

takes but one sense] 'appeals only to one of the senses', probably the sense of touch.

19 *lamely*] feebly. *as*] that.

22] I have inserted a comma after 'lions', and removed one after 'be', as apparently required by the sense of ll. 21–2, viz. 'Alas! why can't we be cheerful . . . just as cocks and lions are?'

21–3] The idea that only the lion and the cock remain brisk after the act of love is at least as old as Galen. Mr T. R. Henn has provided me a

Since so, my mind
Shall not desire what no man else can find;
I'll no more dote and run
To pursue things which had endamag'd me.
And when I come where moving beauties be,
As men do when the summer's sun
Grows great,
Though I admire their greatness, shun their heat;
Each place can afford shadows. If all fail,
'Tis but applying wormseed to the tail.

---

modern reference to Galen's pronouncement, in a poem by Oliver St John Gogarty:

After Galen.
Only the Lion and the Cock,
As Galen says, withstand Love's shock.
So, Dearest, do not think me rude
If I yield now to lassitude,
But sympathize with me. I know
You would not have me roar, or crow.

23–30] A difficult passage, whose interpretation is not made easier by the fact that the poem does not appear in the 1633 edition or in most of the MSS. Mr John Hayward has called the lines 'the most unintelligible in the whole canon of Donne's poetry' (Donne, *Complete Poetry and Selected Prose*, ed. John Hayward, Nonesuch Press, 1949). There would therefore seem to be sufficient excuse for treating the lines at some length. To avoid disproportion, however, I have decided to mention here only some of the more plausible interpretations I have come across, and to give a fuller treatment in an Appendix, for those who may be interested (see Appendix IV, p. 145).

In l. 30 the reading of the 1635–69 editions and of the MSS is:

Eager, desires to raise posterity.

Grierson cleverly emended this to:

Eagers desire to raise posterity.

but his explanation of the emended text does not seem to me satisfactory (see Appendix, p. 145).

One fairly plausible explanation of ll. 23–30 in the original text seems to me to be: 'Unless (since each act of love is said to diminish the length of life a day), wise Nature decreed that men should be melancholy afterwards, because the brevity of sexual play and the momentary character of its climax encourage the repetition of the act.' ('Desires to raise posterity' is here construed as meaning 'desires to raise posterity to the act of love', i.e. encourages its repetition.) (This explanation is a modified form of one suggested in a brilliant note on the poem by Dr George Williamson ('Donne's *Farewell to Love*', *Modern Philology*, 1939, pp. 310–13). A similar explanation was offered by Mr A. M. Coon in *TLS*, 12 Aug. 1939.)

I am, however, very doubtful whether the original reading can stand, and I am strongly attracted by an explanation of the text as amended by Grierson, suggested to me by Mr F. L. Lucas. This is as follows: 'One can only suppose that Nature so ordained (copulation being, as it is, harmful) because she wanted men not to think too much of the act of love: for, on the other hand, the brevity of coitus increases physical desire, so that the race may be perpetuated.' The idea is that Nature has provided both a stimulus and a deterrent to coitus: (1) she has made coitus brief, so that men should wish to repeat it often, and so be fruitful and multiply (if human coitus took a couple of months, as it does with some creatures, clearly the birthrate would be considerably decreased); but (2) lest men should make love too much, she added the melancholy reaction afterwards. Mr Lucas would prefer to add to Grierson's emendation a comma after 'desire', the sense being: 'heightens sexual desire, in order to perpetuate the race', rather than 'heightens the desire to perpetuate the race.'

Mr Lucas's explanation seems to me the best I have yet seen: but I do not feel certain that the matter is entirely closed. If a satisfactory explanation of the original text could be found, that would perhaps be best of all.

Miss Helen Gardner has offered an explanation of a text which differs from the early texts only by the insertion of a comma after 'minute' in l. 29 (*TLS*, 10 June 1949). She takes 'made to be eager' as a transitive verb with 'desires' as its object. The comma after 'eager' she explains as necessary to make us take 'eager' with 'to be' and not with 'desires'. The past tense 'made' was used, in her opinion, because it was that accentuation of our desires which Nature's decree remedied. Miss Gardner's paraphrase is as follows: 'Possibly Nature decreed this after-sorrow to prevent man from destroying himself by repeated indulgence, because that other curse of brevity in enjoyment sharpened or made more acute the natural desires to propagate.' This is also an ingenious explanation, but my objections to it are as follows: (1) that 'and only for a minute' then merely pads out 'of being short', in an un-Donnelike way; and (2) that it seems unnatural to say that the brevity of the act sharpens desire *to raise posterity*. Surely it only sharpens desire *to perform the act again and again*?

31 *Since so*] Since this is the situation.

35 *moving beauties*] devastatingly attractive women.

40 *'Tis but applying*] All that will be necessary will be to apply.

wormseed] wormseed was used as what is generally termed an 'anaphrodisiac' (though 'antaphrodisiac' might really be a better word). Wormseed was prepared from any one of several plants called by that name (e.g. some species of *Artemisia* and *Chenopodium*).

A LECTURE UPON THE SHADOW

Stand still, and I will read to thee
A lecture, love, in love's philosophy.
These three hours that we have spent
In walking here, two shadows went
Along with us, which we ourselves produc'd;
But, now the Sun is just above our head,
We do those shadows tread;
And to brave clearness all things are reduc'd.
So, whilst our infant love did grow,
Disguises did, and shadows, flow
From us, and our cares; but now 'tis not so.

That love hath not attain'd the high'st degree,
Which is still diligent lest others see.

Except our love at this noon stay,
We shall new shadows make the other way.
As the first were made to blind
Others, these which come behind
Will work upon ourselves, and blind our eyes.
If once love faint, and westwardly decline,
To me thou, falsely, thine,
And I to thee mine actions shall disguise.
The morning shadows wear away,
But these grow longer all the day,—
But oh, love's day is short, if love decay.

Love is a growing, or full constant light;
And his first minute, after noon, is night.

A LECTURE UPON THE SHADOW

2 *love*] his lady, not the God of Love, and therefore, in a modern version, better spelt with a small 'l'. Since writing this note I have seen that the late Sir Desmond MacCarthy suggested to Mr John Hayward that the line should read: 'A Lecture, love, in Loves philosophy'. I am slightly disinclined to give a capital to 'love's', because the word then suggests

the god of love: though I would admit that that reading may be correct. Mr Hayward says that the MSS and editions do not support that reading, though he is inclined to think it correct. It is true that the seventeenth-century editions give the reading no support. The 1719 edition, however, does give it partial support by printing: A Lecture, Love, in Love's Philosophie.

8 *brave*] splendid.

9 *love*] After careful consideration I have decided to adopt the reading 'love' in ll. 9, 14, and 19. This is the reading of a large number of MSS, including some of the highest authority. The printed editions 1635–69 read 'loves' (except that in l. 9 the 1669 edition reads 'love'); and this has the support of some MSS, and is the reading adopted by Grierson. My main reason for adopting the reading 'love' is that it is quite clear that Donne is comparing the love between himself and his lady to the sun, and not to the shadows, and that therefore the use of the plural 'loves' risks confusion. Furthermore, no provision is made in the poem for the case where one of the two 'loves' declines, but not the other. The plural, therefore, would not only risk confusion, but would be irrelevant, and I cannot see that it has any compensating advantages.

15 *the other way*] It is perhaps worth considering for a moment which way the shadows fall in the first stanza, and which in the second: as I believe Donne is perhaps laying some stress on the matter of orientation. L. 17 might at first sight seem to make it clear that the shadows in the second stanza fall behind the lovers. On that interpretation, however, what would be the 'disguises' implied by l. 21? They should be like shadows (see l. 10), but the shadows would lie behind the lovers, and be invisible to them. Ll. 19–21, therefore, would suggest that the shadows are now lying in front of the lovers, and growing into more and more fantastically long shapes until they are caught up into the night. In that case, 'come behind' in l. 17 could be interpreted as meaning either (1) that the *source* of the shadows is now behind, or else, as Mr F. L. Lucas has suggested to me, (2) 'come later', taking 'behind' as an adverb of time and not of place. This would accord with 'flow' in l. 10, which suggests that the shadows are behind the lovers in stanza 1. There the shadows were left to baffle others: after noon they would lie in front, and baffle the lovers themselves.

19 *If once love faint*] I have ventured to adopt this reading of a number of MSS, including several of the highest authority, in preference to the reading of the 1635–69 editions, and some other MSS: 'If our loves faint', partly for the reasons mentioned in my note on l. 9 above, and partly because 'once' seems to me a more pointed word than the rather tame 'our', and also to fit in better with the epigrammatic ending in ll. 25–6.

faint] grows less powerful.

24] The drift seems to be: 'But, alas, there wouldn't even be the chance of the shadows growing longer and longer in *love's* afternoon; for it is too short!'

(SONNET) THE TOKEN

Send me some token, that my hope may live,
  Or that my easeless thoughts may sleep and rest;
Send me some honey to make sweet my hive,
  That in my passion I may hope the best.
I beg no riband wrought with thine own hands,
  To knit our loves in the fantastic strain
Of new-touch'd youth; nor ring to shew the stands
  Of our affection, that, as that's round and plain,
So should our loves meet in simplicity:
  No, nor the corals which thy wrist enfold,
Lac'd up together in congruity,
  To shew our thoughts should rest in the same hold:
No, nor thy picture, though most gracious,
  And most desir'd, because best like the best;
Nor witty lines, which are most copious
  Within the writings which thou hast address'd.

  Send me nor this nor that to increase my store,
  But swear thou think'st I love thee, and no more.

(SONNET) THE TOKEN

General Note: I have included this poem, because I am following Professor Grierson in matters of canon. The poem does not, however, seem to me typical of Donne, though I have no positive evidence against its authenticity. It was first printed in the 1649 edition, and does not appear in many of the most authoritative MSS.

Note on the title: The poem is clearly not a sonnet in the sense in which the term is now used. The title in the old printed editions 1649–69 is, however: '*Sonnet. The Token.*' To preserve the old title, with its indication of the old usage of the term 'sonnet', and its accord with the title of this volume, and at the same time to avoid causing confusion, I have retained the word 'Sonnet', but enclosed it in brackets.

7 *new-touch'd*] newly touched by love.
stands] standing.
11 *in congruity*] so as to fit perfectly.
12 *rest in the same hold*] be bound up together just as closely.
13 *gracious*] trisyllabic.

16 *address'd*] written.

18 *and no more*] and that's all.

< THE REJECTION >
or
< SELF-LOVE >

He that cannot choose but love,
And strives against it still,
Never shall my fancy move,
For he loves against his will;
Nor he which is all his own,
And can at pleasure choose,—
When I am caught he can be gone,
And, when he list, refuse;
Nor he that loves none but fair,
For such by all are sought;
Nor he that can for foul ones care,
For his judgment then is nought;
Nor he that hath wit, for he
Will make me his jest or slave;
Nor a fool, for when others . . . ,
He can neither . . . . ;
Nor he that still his mistress pays,
For she is thrall'd therefore:
Nor he that pays not, for he says
Within, she's worth no more.
Is there then no kind of men
Whom I may freely prove ?
I will vent that humour then
In mine own self-love.

⟨THE REJECTION⟩ or ⟨SELF-LOVE⟩

Note on the title: This poem bears no title either in the 1650–69 editions or in the MSS in which it appears. Sir Edmund Chambers gave it the title *Self-love*. This title is in some ways appropriate, and it has the advantage of being rather witty as a title to this particular poem: but it does not cover another important aspect of the poem, namely the rejection, by the woman into whose mouth the poem is put, of the various types of lover. This rejection, moreover, seems to be based on a consideration of each type of lover on his merits, and not to be *merely* a rationalization of self-love, though it may well indeed be partly this. I have therefore ventured to introduce the title *The Rejection*, retaining Chambers's title as an alternative, partly because I think that both titles contribute to an understanding of the poem, and partly because Chambers's title has already acquired further currency through its adoption both by Professor Grierson and by a number of plain-text editors.

Note on the layout: In a letter to *TLS*, 21 Dec. 1956, Mr John Sparrow makes the interesting suggestion that it might be better to print this poem as six quatrains. This would certainly, as he observes, bring out its song-like character. I have been sorely tempted to adopt this suggestion, but have decided against it on two grounds: (1) The lack of support for it in the MSS and old editions; (2) the fact that four of the six quatrains would end in stops lighter than a full-stop, a proportion without parallel in the *Songs and Sonets*. Mr Sparrow's suggestion does, however, in any case, draw attention to a feature of the poem which is important, and which the traditional layout tends to obscure.

5] Nor he who is completely self-possessed.

8 *refuse*] probably: 'refuse to make love to me'.

9 *fair*] beautiful women.

15–16] I have made no attempt to fill in this gap in the text: though the number of possible combinations does not seem immense. I have investigated many, but without satisfaction. A poetically sensitive crossword puzzle expert might well achieve the restoration! The best attempt I have myself made is:

Nor a fool, for when others see,
He can neither rest nor rave, . . .

It is, of course, possible that Donne himself never completed the lines, and even conceivable that, if he did not, it was because he could find no satisfactory words to fill them!

18] For that makes her a slave.

20 *Within*] to himself.

22 *prove*] approve.

23 *that humour*] i.e. the inclination to approve.

Appendix I

Note on Introduction, p. xlviii

Would Donne's revised text necessarily be the authentic text?

Supposing that revisions by Donne himself did take place, whether at 1614 or at any other time, what should we consider as 'the authentic text'? The revised version or the unrevised version? For instance, in *The Will*, the third stanza is omitted in manuscripts of Groups I and II, but appears in certain manuscripts of Group III, one of which (the Stephens MS) is dated 1620, and contains no poems demonstrably later than 1610. This makes it likely that the stanza appeared in an early version of the poem. But it could well have proved offensive from a religious point of view; and it is therefore probable that Donne deliberately dropped it. Which should we regard as the authentic text in this case, that which excludes the stanza or that which includes it? It is a problem not altogether dissimilar to that presented by the 1805 and 1850 versions of Wordsworth's *Prelude*. The seventeenth-century editors print the stanza, and Grierson follows them. He does so of deliberate policy, since his text is based on the 1633 edition: but the teasing question remains, whether that edition itself represents the authentic text in this case. Here, it is worth noting, Grierson has followed the 'unrevised' text. Another interesting case, by way of contrast, is that of l. 24 in *The Damp*, which in Group I manuscripts reads: Naked you've odds enough of any man. In Group II manuscripts 'Naked' appears as 'In that', a probable revision intended to tone the line down. A number of Group III manuscripts, including the Stephens MS, read 'Naked': and this seems to confirm that 'Naked' was the earlier version. In this case the 1633 edition reads: 'In that'; while the 1635 edition reverts to 'Naked', and the remaining seventeenth-century editions keep that reading. Grierson again follows the 1633 edition: but in doing so he has, in fact, followed what is probably the 'revised', as opposed to the 'unrevised' text. His rather strict following of the 1633 edition, therefore, does lead Grierson to follow sometimes what seems to be an 'unrevised' text, and sometimes what seems to be a 'revised' text. I believe that Grierson was very probably right to make the 1633 edition the basis of his text; and that his text is the best so far; but I also believe that occasionally his text does not make sufficient concession to 'unrevised' versions, where it can be seen that the 'revisions' were probably made for reasons extraneous to the value of the poems as works of art. The mere fact that the 1633 edition does not adopt a particular 'unrevised' version should not, in my view, be regarded as binding; especially when we bear in mind the fact that it does sometimes adopt such versions.

APPENDIX II

'Specular Stone'

(*The Undertaking, l. 6*)

Norton (Grolier Edition, i. 217), rightly, in my view, took 'specular stone' to be the 'pierre spéculaire' described by Cotgrave: 'A light, white, and transparent stone, easily cleft into thinne flakes, and used by th' Arabians (among whom it growes) instead of glasse; anight it represents the Moon, and even increases or decreases as the Moon doth'. Norton did not, however, fully explain the whole phrase 'the skill of specular stone'.

Chambers and Grierson both took the whole phrase to refer to the art of crystal-gazing; though Grierson confessed himself baffled by 'the reference to the cutting of the stone on the one hand, and its being no longer to be found, on the other'.

Much light has been thrown on these points by Professor Don Cameron Allen in his note entitled 'Donne's *Specular Stone*', published in *Modern Language Notes*, January 1946, at pp. 63–4. He refers to *Seminarum et lapidum historia* (1609) by Anselmus Boetius de Boot, which he calls 'the first modern mineralogy'. There the properties of selenite, as recorded by Pliny, Galen, Dioscorides, and Albertus Magnus, are summarized in ch. 215, where it is also stated that the stone has not been found 'since ancient times'. The treatise states that 'specular stone' is considered by many writers to be the modern counterpart of selenite. Boetius describes the 'specular stone' as follows: 'This stone is as clear as crystal, and is cut into very thin sheets, thinner than any ordinary paper, without on that account losing its transparency. . . It can be used in lanterns and windows just like glass.'

In the light of his findings Professor Allen suggests what seems to me the right explanation of our phrase and stanza. The 'skill' he takes to be either (1) the 'division' of the stone into sheets (which seems to me unlikely, since the *noun* 'skill' was not currently used in the sense of 'separation' or 'division'), or (2), I think more plausibly, the *method* of dividing it. (I should myself prefer to take it to mean 'the craft of dividing it'.)

On the other hand, it seems to me that further support is required before the explanation can be regarded as watertight: for Donne does speak simply of 'specular stone', and we cannot conclude from that alone whether he meant old selenite or its modern counterpart. I believe the further support required can be found in the fact that Donne, when he uses the term 'specular stone' elsewhere, is almost certainly referring to old selenite rather than to its modern counterpart. Let us consider the lines referring to 'specular stone' in Donne's *Letter to the Countess of Bedford* (Grierson, I. 219), ll. 28–30:

You teach (though wee learne not) a thing unknowne
To our late times, the use of specular stone,
Through which all things within without were shown.

These lines are explained by Professor Allen, I believe rightly, as referring to the use of specular stone for glazing. The point I wish to make, however, is that here by 'specular stone' Donne must mean the ancient stone, probably old selenite. A striking confirmation of Professor Allen's interpretation of these lines, and some support for my own point, is to be found in a passage from one of Donne's Sermons (Sermon 27 of *Fifty Sermons: Donne's Prose Works*, ed. Alford, IV. 472–3): 'The heathens served their gods in temples, *sub dio*, without roofs or coverings, in a free openness; and, where they could, in temples made of specular-stone, that was transparent as glass, or crystal, so as they which walked without in the streets, might see all that was done within.' It may well be that Donne, when he wrote the poem, knew nothing of any modern counterpart to the old stone.

APPENDIX III

Air and Angels (ll. 24, 26–8)

24 *it*] It is a vexed point whether 'it' refers back to 'Angel' (l. 23) or to 'air' (l. 24). The main arguments against the view that 'it' refers back to Angel are (1) that that would be bad syntax, since the pronoun would naturally refer to the last noun before it; (2) that it would be bad angelology, since in the Bible angels were always referred to as male: and that it would be contrary to Donne's own usage, since he accepts the Biblical practice; (3) that Donne is referring in the poem to the Thomist doctrine that angels manifest themselves to men by taking on bodies of *specially condensed* air; and that to switch attention from that point to an utterly different one, viz. the difference in purity between incorporeal angels and the bodies they take on, would be to cloud the sense of the poem. (These arguments are put forward with great force in an unpublished note on the poem by Mr Hugh Sykes Davies, Fellow of St John's College. I am indebted to him for the loan of this note.)

In my view, the most substantial of these arguments is (2). As to (1), Donne's practice in matters of syntax is flexible: there are other cases in his work in which the pronoun 'it' is not used to refer to the last noun before it. Moreover, if 'it' referred back to 'air', what kind of air would it be referring to? It could not be to uncondensed air, for that was not the kind of air in which angels were supposed to be bodily manifested. Nor could it be to condensed air, for then Donne would be saying that condensed air is not as pure as condensed air, which is absurd.

As to (3), I for one should not be willing to concede that attention is concentrated in the poem on the point of Thomist doctrine that the air of the bodies assumed by angels is *condensed*. There is, therefore, in my view, no question of *switching* attention *from* that point. It would seem to me, on the contrary, that if at all, it is only in this one line (l. 24) that that specific point is referred to, and that the reference is merely parenthetical. The poem as a whole, in so far as it lives up to its title, seems to me to be concerned with air and angels, not with two kinds of air, one rarefied and one condensed. I find no evidence of the specific doctrine elsewhere in the poem at all. Again, the relevant passage from St Thomas Aquinas (*Summa Theol.*, I. li. 2), quoted by Grierson, does not say that the condensed air of an angel's body is less *pure* than rarefied air: it simply says that it is thicker. Now honey, for example, can be just as 'pure' whether it is thick or thin. There is, therefore, at least one sense of 'pure' in which condensed air would be as pure as rarefied air. It is admittedly possible that Donne means here by 'pure', *clear*, not *free from impurities*. Yet I see no reason to suppose that that is what he does mean. Moreover, the adjective 'pure' could properly be applied in Donne's time to the physical state of an angel before taking on an airy body. Grierson, in his note (II.21) quotes a passage from Tasso, in which Gabriel is said to take on a body of air:

> La sua forma invisibil d'aria cinse,
> Ed al senso mortal la sottopose: . . .

Now Fairfax translates these lines as follows:

> In form of airy members fair imbared,
> His spirits pure were subject to our sight.

Here the term 'pure' clearly refers to the incorporeal state of the angel. May it not be, then, that even if 'it' refers to 'Angel', Donne is not parting company with Thomist doctrine, but simply referring to that part of it which teaches that angels, which are pure spirits, take on bodies of air which are not as pure as their spirits are, but are pure compared with other bodies, e.g. bodies composed of more than one element?

If this point is valid, the only outstanding objection to the view that 'it' refers to 'Angel' is that of the sex of angels (argument 2). I do not now find this to be a strong objection: but I do think it worth consideration. Elsewhere Donne sometimes refers to angels as male, occasionally as female, but most often refers to them without indication of sex. I am indebted to Mr Robin Wilson of Trinity College for urging me to re-consider the evidence against argument (2), and for collecting for me a considerable number of instances of Donne's use of the term 'angel'. He rightly lays stress on ll. 25–6 of *The Relic*:

> Difference of sex we never knew,
> No more than our guardian angels do; . . .

This *could* indeed be interpreted as meaning that all guardian angels were male: but taking the passage within Donne's system of usage I believe the correct interpretation to be that Donne thought of angels as sexless, or, more strictly, as beings to whom *per se*, in virtue of their incorporeality, the attribute of sex was wholly irrelevant. That angels were *per se* incorporeal was the considered view of such authorities as Dionysius the Areopagite and St Thomas Aquinas. There does seem, moreover, to be an additional objection to the view that 'it' refers to air, namely this: Suppose that the last three lines of the poem are suggesting that men's love corresponds to the angel, and women's love to the air of the angel's body, then to interpret 'it' in l. 24 to refer to 'air' would result in a line which makes a great deal of fuss about a supposed difference in 'purity' between rare and condensed air, which would have no relevance to the last three lines, and might well cause great confusion to a reader. Clearly, though, this objection would have no force at all unless the last three lines do suggest that men's love corresponds to the angel, and women's love to the air of the angel's body. It will therefore be proper to postpone final judgement on this objection till ll. 26–8 have been considered.

To sum up I should say: (*a*) that logical syntax strongly favours the view that 'it' refers to 'Angel'; (*b*) that in correct usage rarefied air would not be 'purer' than condensed air; (*c*) (i) that there is support elsewhere in Donne for the view that he concurred with high theological authority in holding that angels were *per se* incorporeal, and (ii) that it would naturally follow that in his view they had *per se* no sex. The upshot is that I think there is in any case a definite preponderance of support for the view that 'it' refers back to 'Angel'.

26–8] I should argue for the view that these lines imply that men's love is purer than women's, as follows: (1) If the phrase 'Just such disparity' (in l. 26) refers *back*, it would be most natural to take it to refer to the 'disparity' between the angel and its body, which has been the subject of the immediately preceding three lines taken as a whole, rather than to refer to the 'disparity' between rarefied and condensed air, which, if referred to at all in the poem, is at most the subject of a parenthetical reference in l. 24 only, which is separated by a whole line from the phrase 'Just such disparity' in l. 26. If this point is valid, then it is obvious that l. 27 would most probably refer to the disparity between the angel and air in respect of purity: and not to the disparity between rare and condensed air. It might be contended (though, in my opinion, not very convincingly) that the words 'Just such disparity' in l. 26 do not refer back at all, but only forward: and that therefore argument (1) carries no weight. While not accepting the premises of this objection, I should go on to make an independent point:

(2) Even if we were to take 'it' in l. 24 to refer to 'air', the main point of ll. 23–5 would still be that the woman's love can be the *sphere* of Donne's (the element in which it works, or the sphere which it controls: both meanings are possible). The meaning of ll. 23–5 in that case would be: 'So the solution will have to be that just as an angel takes on a face and wings of air (not rarefied air, but pure air all the same), so my love must assume your *love* as its body, or, to vary the metaphor, my love must take your love as its sphere, just as an angel exerts control over a sphere' [*or*, if we take 'sphere' to mean *element*: 'so my love must assume your love as the body or element in which it can act']. That is, however we take 'sphere', the relationships will be these: 'The poet's love must be to his lady's love as the angel is to the body that it takes on.'

Now the next step in my argument would be that whatever else there is reason to suppose the last three lines of the poem to be doing, there is certainly no reason to suppose that they are contradicting the three previous lines or blurring the comparison already made in them. Ll. 26–8 are pointing to a perennial distinction between women's love and men's. If this perennial distinction were a wholly different one from the difference between Donne's love and his lady's, which has been indicated in ll. 23–5, then that comparison would be blurred. It would scarcely be a caricature to say that what would be happening would be that Donne would be saying: 'My love must be to your love as an angel is to the body it assumes; and, as a matter of fact, women's love perennially differs from men's love in the same way in which pure air differs from the body of an angel'; which would be, I suggest, a complete *non sequitur*.

In contrast, there would be no hitch at all if we were to interpret the points made in the last six lines of the poem as being these: 'My love must be to your love as the angel is to the body it assumes: and, as a matter of fact, the *perennial* distinction between women's love and men's is that women's is like the aerial body whereas men's is like the angel itself.' I would insist here on the word 'ever' in the last line, which would seem to me only to have point if the last three lines are an appeal to a generalization within which Donne's own case falls.

(3) Finally, I would also urge that to interpret the last three lines as referring to a distinction between the purity of an angel before it takes on a body, and the purity of that body, fits better the general sense of the poem. Donne's love, the man's love, is to take a body (l. 10). It fails at first to find a satisfactory body: then it finds one. It did not have a body to begin with, or the search would be pointless. The original state of the man's love is therefore bodiless, and this fits the comparison with the angel, for the angel is also originally bodiless. St Thomas Aquinas clearly maintained this (see e.g. the Opusculum *De Substantiis Separatis* (Opuscula Omnia ed. Mandonnet, Paris, 1927, pp. 70–144)). If, then, the last three lines of the poem are referring to the natural bodiless character of angels, they would be emphasizing a fundamental point in Thomist angelology; and an important point in the comparison between Donne's originally bodiless love and the originally bodiless angel; and they would also be performing a very proper function in harking back to the first stanza.

These, then, are my reasons for believing that the last three lines of the poem imply that men's love is purer than women's. This is not necessarily a cynical touch on Donne's part, though. Women's love is also called 'pure' by implication. I should rather regard the statement as a gentle piece of badinage.

24] We may now return to l. 24, and attempt, as promised, a decision on the last objection to the view that 'it' refers back to 'air'. If my view of ll. 26–8 is correct, then it would seem disproportionate for Donne to mention in l. 24 a difference between the purity of condensed and rarefied air, in view of what would then be its irrelevance to ll. 26–8. Could one meet this objection in any way? Could one give some point to l. 24 which would not make it a disproportionate fuss? I think one *might* be able to. Ll. 23–4 say that the face and wings of the angel are made of *air*: this is part of the main point Donne wishes to make; but then, with the live mind he had, he might have seen that someone might make the niggling objection that this air is not ordinary pure air, but something less pure, and therefore not a fit image for women's love; and so he might have wished to knock the bottom out of this objection once for all by conceding that the air of the angel's body was not as pure as ordinary air, while maintaining that it was pure all the same. That would *perhaps* be a *possible* interpretation were this the only objection to the view that 'it' refers back to 'air'. But, in any case, I am convinced that it is not in fact the true interpretation, since the total case against 'it' referring back to 'air' seems to me so strong.

APPENDIX IV

Farewell to Love (ll. 23–30)

For the reader who is interested the following is an account of some of the principal suggestions which have been made as to the meaning of the passage. For the sake of completeness the present note will to some extent repeat points made in the body of the Notes.

Grierson (op. cit., II. 53) explains the whole stanza, as amended by him, as follows: 'Donne's argument then is this: "Why of all animals have we alone this feeling of depression and remorse after the act of love? Is it a device of nature to restrain us from an act which shortens the life of the individual" (he refers here to a prevalent belief as to the deleterious effect of the act of love), "needed because that other curse which Adam brought upon man, the curse of mortality,

> Of being short,
> And only for a minute made to be,
> Eagers [i.e. whets or provokes] desire to raise posterity?"'

My own view is that, apart from the fact that if possible one should keep the old reading, Grierson's emendation is open to a strong objection, namely that it does not seem like Donne to pad in l. 29 by practically repeating the sense of l. 28.

Mr John Hayward, in the Nonesuch Donne (pp. 766–7), has also suggested an emendation, which consists in transposing the comma in l. 30 from after 'eager' to after 'desires', so that the line would read:

> Eager desires, to raise posterity.

Mr Hayward objects to Grierson's emendation and explanation (1) that it would destroy a rhythm characteristic of Donne (I do not accept that point); (2) that he cannot agree that 'That other curse of being short, And only for a minute made to be', refers to the curse of mortality brought upon man by Adam. (That is a crucial point which I shall deal with below.) Mr Hayward thinks these lines (ll. 28–9) refer to the short ecstasy of physical union. His third objection to Grierson's view is: (3) that it is hard to see why, if the curse of mortality stimulates desire to raise posterity, Nature should decree that man should despise that very reasonable desire. (My own answer to this would be that Donne would not be saying, on Grierson's view, that Nature has perhaps decreed that man should despise that desire, but only that Nature has perhaps decreed that man should despise the *sport* of sexuality.)

On the basis of his own view that ll. 28–9 refer to the short ecstasy of physical union, Mr Hayward explains the stanza as follows: 'Unlike the beasts, man feels sad after the act of love. Why is this? Nature decreed that it should be so, and would have man despise the sport of raising posterity since the act itself is short and the desires that promote it are made eager by nature for a moment only; moreover, it is said that each such act diminishes the length of life a day.'

My objections to Mr Hayward's emendation and explanation are as follows: (1) that if good sense can be given to the old reading, it should clearly be preferred; (2) that ll. 29–30, as amended by Mr Hayward, seem to me less characteristic of Donne than ll. 29–30 as amended by Professor Grierson; (3) that there is no question in the poem of man despising 'the sport of raising posterity'; (4) that Donne is not suggesting in ll. 28–30 features of the 'sport' in virtue of which man ought to despise it, but either reasons for nature's decree or reasons why man or the act of love desires 'to raise posterity'; (5) that Mr Hayward puts the point about diminution of life at the end, and his explanation does not bring out the fact that this is the reason Donne attributes to Nature for making her decree.

Ever since I first considered the knotty problem set by this passage, I had thought that a good sense might be given to the old reading. I myself at first accepted a modified form of Grierson's view about the meaning of 'That other curse', viz. that it referred to humanity's living only for a short while and only for a mere minute at a high pitch of life. On this interpretation I still think that sense might be given to the old reading, viz: 'since humanity's other curse of living only for a short while, and only for a mere minute at a high pitch of life, makes men long to have children'. My own objection to this reading and explanation was that it involved rather vigorous construction of the word 'desires', perhaps too vigorous even for Donne's work.

After reading, however, the positively brilliant note on the poem by Dr George Williamson ('Donne's *Farewell to Love*', in *Modern Philology*, 1939, pp. 301–3), I came round to the view that Mr Hayward was probably right, as against Professor Grierson, in maintaining that 'That other curse' was the brevity of sexual play. Dr Williamson accepts Mr Hayward's view on this point: but he makes an ingenious addition, viz. the view that 'to raise posterity' has nothing to do with humanity's begetting of children, but refers to the fact that the act of love itself, because of its shortness and only momentary sharpness, wishes to repeat itself (i.e. 'raise posterity' *to itself*). Dr Williamson suggests that the meaning of the whole stanza is as follows: 'If it be not that (since each such act, they say, diminishes the length of life a day) wise Nature decreed this, as if she would that man should despise the sport [not that she does]; because that other curse of being short, and but momentarily eager, desires to raise posterity [i.e. desires to increase and multiply, for only by multiplying itself can the curse of shortness and momentary ardour escape its limitations].' Dr Williamson also explains that this other curse of love provides the reason for the necessity of Nature's decree, not the reason for despising the sport. The decree itself is what provides a reason for despising the sport, since the mere brevity of the experience is not sufficient to discourage people from indulging in it. In fact the brevity has the opposite effect, and that is why Nature needs to provide the safeguard of 'sorrowing dulness'. The fundamental reason, however, why Nature makes her decree, is suggested in the parenthesis. It is because Nature is concerned to preserve human life, and so wishes to discourage excessive sexuality. Of course Nature is interested in multiplying life as well as preserving it, a fact which is allowed for in the 'as if' mood of Donne's reasoning about her, but which is not in issue in the poem. Nature achieves both objects by subjecting man to the two curses of love, which hinder each other: the curse of brevity demands continual repetition, the curse of a dull aftermath produces eternal dissatisfaction. And so the only solution for a man concerned for his own happiness is to renounce love. And that brings out the significance of the title of the poem, *Farewell to Love.*

This ingenious interpretation has attractive features. In particular, the reserved subtlety of l. 30, as so explained, seems truly worthy of Donne at his best. The interpretation is, however, open to certain objections, as we shall see.

Ten years later Dr Leslie Hotson also attempted (in *TLS*, 16 April 1949) an explanation of the original text. He took 'that other curse' to refer to the curse of mortality, and suggested that 'because' (l. 28) is here used to refer to the future, with the force 'in order that' (see Abbott, *Shakespearian Grammar*, § 117), the sense being 'in order that man should desire to raise posterity'. He was, however, unable to cite an *exact* parallel for this use of 'because'. His explanation also seems to me to miss the point that the primary reason for Nature's decree was that the act of love diminishes the length of human life.

Shoftly afterwards Miss Helen Gardner wrote a note (in *TLS*, 10 June 1949) rejecting Dr Leslie Hotson's explanation, and also attacking Dr Williamson's interpretation on the grounds (1) that it is improbable that Donne would use the phrase 'raise posterity' in that metaphorical way in a poem concerned with the very act by which posterity is raised in the ordinary sense; (2) that 'that other curse' is not the subject of 'desires', which is indeed not a verb here at all. Of these objections (1) seems to me by far the stronger. It seems to me by no means certain that 'desires' is not a verb, and indeed that is, in any case, one of the points at issue. Miss Gardner also put forward her own explanation, which involves the insertion of a comma after 'minute' in l. 29. She takes 'made to be eager' as a transitive verb with 'desires' as its object. She holds that the comma after 'eager' in the original text is necessary to make us take 'eager' with 'to be' and not with 'desires': and that the past tense 'made' is used because it was this accentuation of our desires which Nature's decree remedied. Her paraphrase is as follows: 'Possibly Nature decreed this after-sorrow to prevent man from destroying himself by repeated indulgence, because that other curse of brevity in enjoyment sharpened or made more acute the natural desires to propagate.' This explanation has distinct attractions; but it does seem to me open to the following objections: (1) that 'and only for a minute' would then simply pad out 'of being short', which would not be typical of Donne: and (2) that it seems unnatural to say that the brevity of the act sharpens desire *to raise posterity*. What it *does* sharpen would seem to be desire *to perform the act*.

Mr F. L. Lucas has recently drawn my attention to some possible objections to Dr Williamson's explanation, and he has also provided me with an attractive explanation of his own, involving Grierson's emendation, which he considers 'more convincing than most such conjectures are'. Mr Lucas takes the shortness referred to in l. 28 to be that of coitus. On the other hand, he objects to the phrase 'desires to raise posterity' in the original text being taken to mean 'wishes to repeat itself', on the ground that the subject of 'desires' is not the *act*, but the *curse*. He also considers Dr Williamson's interpretation of 'to raise posterity' forced. His own explanation of the passage (from 'Unless wise Nature . . .') is as follows: 'One can only suppose that Nature so ordained (copulation being, as it is, harmful) because she wanted men not to think *too* much of the act of love: for, on the other hand, the brevity of coitus increases physical desire, so that the race may be perpetuated.' The idea is that Nature has provided both a stimulus and a deterrent to coitus. (1) She has made coitus *brief*, so that men should wish to repeat it often, and so be fruitful and multiply. (If human coitus took a couple of months, as it does with some creatures, clearly the birthrate would be considerably decreased.) But (2) lest men should make love *too* much, she added the melancholy reaction afterwards. Mr Lucas would prefer to add to Grierson's emendation a comma after 'desire', the sense being: 'heightens sexual desire, in order to perpetuate the race', rather than 'heightens the desire to perpetuate the race'.

The objections made to Dr Williamson's interpretation by Miss Gardner and Mr Lucas clearly have some force. I am personally most strongly impressed by Miss Gardner's first objection, though, of course, one cannot rule out the possibility of an 'evaporation of wit' at this point. The other objections seem to me all more or less readily answerable. I do not, in any case, feel that any of the objections is conclusive, and Dr Williamson's interpretation therefore seems to me still worth consideration, at least in the modified form suggested in my note (p. 131). It certainly avoids the 'padding' objection which appears to lie against practically all the other interpretations.

As to Mr Lucas's own interpretation, it seems to me, despite three drawbacks, to be the most satisfactory of those yet proposed. The three drawbacks are: (1) that it involves an emended text; (2) that it does not meet the objection I made early in this note against Grierson's emendation itself, namely that it makes l. 29 into mere padding which repeats what has already been said with scarcely any addition. Mr Lucas calls the whole sexual process referred to 'the coitus', but one seems to want to reserve l. 29 to refer to the coitus itself, and to take l. 28 to refer to the whole sexual play within which coitus falls: on the original reading this distinction is easily made; (3) that the phrase 'to raise posterity' seems to stand in an isolation not typical of Donne's syntax. On the other hand, Mr Lucas's interpretation makes excellent sense: and it succeeds in combining the interpretation of ll. 28–9 as referring to sexuality and not life, with the interpretation of 'to raise posterity' in its most natural sense. It also avoids my second objection to Miss Gardner's interpretation. These are no mean advantages. The matter, however, does not seem to me to be closed.

SELECT BIBLIOGRAPHY

For fuller information the reader is referred to Sir Geoffrey Keynes's *Bibliography of Dr John Donne*, Cambridge, 1958; also the bibliography in *Studies in Metaphysical Poetry*, by T. Spencer and M. Van Doren, Cambridge, U.S.A., 1939; and to William White's *John Donne since 1900: A Bibliography of Periodical Articles* (Boston, 1942). *The Year's Work in English Studies* provides a useful guide to the leading current work.

I. SOME OF THE CHIEF MODERN EDITIONS OF THE POEMS

The Poems of John Donne, ed. H. J. C. Grierson, with Introductions and Commentary, 2 vols., Oxford, 1912. (The standard text, in old spelling, with critical and textual introductions, critical apparatus, and many explanatory notes.)

The Poems of John Donne, ed. H. J. C. Grierson, Oxford, 1929. (A plain text in old spelling, in the series of Oxford Standard Authors; containing an Introduction and selected textual apparatus.)

The Complete Poems of John Donne, ed. Roger E. Bennett, Chicago University Press, 1942. (A plain text in modern spelling, embodying original study of manuscripts.)

Complete Poetry and Selected Prose, ed. John Hayward, The Nonesuch Press, London, 1929. (The complete poems and an excellent selection from the prose, all in old spelling; based on original study of the old editions and many manuscripts; and with a few explanatory notes.)

Metaphysical Lyrics and Poems of the Seventeenth Century (*Donne to Butler*), selected and ed., with an Introductory Essay, by H. J. C. Grierson, Oxford, 1921. (Contains a number of Donne's poems, in old spelling, with a few explanatory notes. There is also a very useful Introduction covering the whole scope of metaphysical poetry.)

Selected Poems, ed. John Hayward, Penguin Poets, 1950. (A plain text in old spelling, with a short Introduction and a very few notes.)

Selected Poetry and Prose, Walton's Life, and critical observations by Jonson, Dryden, Coleridge and others, ed. (with an Introduction) by H. W. Garrod, Oxford, 1946. (A good small selection in old spelling in the Clarendon Press series, with some notes and a brief Introduction.)

Selected Poems, ed. with notes by James Reeves, Heinemann, London, 1952. (A selection in old spelling, with attempts at paraphrase and a few other notes.)

The Poems of John Donne, ed. H. I'A. Fausset, Everyman Library, London, 1931. (A plain text in modern spelling, with a short Introduction.)

The Divine Poems, ed., with an Introduction and Notes, by Helen Gardner, Oxford, 1953. (An outstanding *editio major* of *The Divine Poems*, with revised text, in old spelling, critical and textual Introduction, full critical apparatus, and thorough explanatory notes.)

Poèmes choisis, Traduction, introduction et notes par Pierre Legouis, Paris, n.d. [1955]. (A well-chosen selection, scrupulously translated, briefly annotated, and with a full general introduction.)

II. A FEW MODERN EDITIONS OF PROSE WORK

Complete Poetry and Selected Prose, ed. John Hayward, The Nonesuch Press, 1929. (Worth mentioning again for its excellent selection from the prose.)

Sermons: Selected Passages with an Essay and Notes, ed. Logan Pearsall Smith, Oxford, 1919.

Sermons, ed. G. R. Potter and E. M. Simpson, 10 vols. (in course of publication), Univ. of California Press, 1953—. (Seven vols. have so far appeared, Vol. I, 1953; Vol. VI, 1953; Vol. VII, 1954; Vol. II, 1955; Vol. VIII, 1956; Vol. III, 1957; Vol. IX, 1958.)

Devotions, ed. John Sparrow, Cambridge, 1923.

Paradoxes and Problems or *Juvenilia*, ed. G. Keynes, Nonesuch Press, London, 1923.

Essays in Divinity, ed. E. M. Simpson, Oxford, 1952.

Biathanatos, reprinted in facsimile, from first edn. (1646), by the Facsimile Text Society, ed. J. W. Hebel, New York, 1930.

The *Pseudo-Martyr* has not been reprinted since 1610.

A fair selection of *Letters* is included in the Nonesuch Donne (see above). Mr I. A. Shapiro is at present working on an edition of the *Letters*.

On all aspects of the prose works the reader should consult E. M. Simpson —*A Study of the Prose Works of John Donne*, Oxford, 1924; 2nd edn., 1948.

III. BIOGRAPHY

Life, by Izaak Walton, 1640; enlarged, 1658. (There is a useful reprint in The World's Classics, Oxford, 1927.)

Sir Edmund Gosse, *Life and Letters of John Donne* (2 vols., London, 1899). (Still the standard biography, but to be treated with great caution, both on account of its imaginative character, and in the light of subsequent research.)

Professor R. C. Bald, of the University of Chicago, is now preparing what should prove the new standard biography.

There is a useful sketch of Donne's Life in Ch. II of E. M. Simpson's *A Study of the Prose Works of John Donne*, 2nd edn., 1948.

There have been a great many articles on points in Donne's biography, notably by Professors F. P. Wilson, H. W. Garrod, R. C. Bald, Roger E. Bennett, George Williamson, G. C. Moore Smith, and W. Milgate, Dr John Sampson, Messrs John Sparrow and I. A. Shapiro, and Mrs E. M. Simpson. Those interested are referred to the bibliographical material already cited.

IV. SOME CRITICAL STUDIES

A. Books and essays

JOAN BENNETT. *Four Metaphysical Poets*, Cambridge, 1934.

'The Love Poetry of John Donne—A Reply to Mr C. S. Lewis', in *Seventeenth Century Studies presented to Sir Herbert Grierson*, Oxford, 1938.

C. M. COFFIN. *John Donne and the New Philosophy*, New York, 1937.

R. G. COX. 'The Poems of Donne', in *From Donne to Marvell*, ed. B. Ford, Penguin Books, 1956.

E. DOWDEN. Essay on Donne in *New Studies in English Literature*, London, 1895.

T. S. ELIOT. 'The Metaphysical Poets' (1921), included in *Selected Essays*.

H. I'A. FAUSSET. *John Donne*, London, 1924.

R. FREEMAN. *English Emblem Books*, London, 1948.

H. J. C. GRIERSON. 'The Poetry of Donne', in Vol. II of Donne's Poetical Works, ed. Grierson, Oxford, 1912.

Introduction to *Metaphysical Lyrics and Poems of the Seventeenth Century*, ed. Grierson, Oxford, 1921.

Article on Donne in *The Cambridge History of English Literature*, 1909. The article is in Vol. VII.

E. HARDY. *John Donne: a spirit in conflict*, London, 1942.

M. HASAN. *Donne's Imagery*, Aligarh, India, 1958.

M. Y. HUGHES. 'Kidnapping Donne' (in *Essays in Criticism, Second Series*, University of California Press, and Cambridge University Press, 1934).

C. HUNT. *Donne's Poetry: Essays in Literary Analysis*, Yale U.P., 1954.

F. R. LEAVIS. *Revaluation*, London, 1936.

J. B. LEISHMAN. *The Metaphysical Poets*, Oxford, 1934.

The Monarch of Wit, London, 1951.

P. LEGOUIS. *Donne the Craftsman*, Paris, 1928.

C. S. LEWIS. 'Donne and Love Poetry in the Seventeenth Century' (in the same volume as Joan Bennett's essay).

G. R. POTTER. 'John Donne's Discovery of Himself' (in the same volume as M. Y. Hughes's essay).

M. PRAZ. *Secentismo e Marinismo in Inghilterra*, Florence, 1925, revised edn., Rome, 1948.

Studies in Seventeenth Century Imagery, London, 1939.

La poesia metafisica inglese del Secento—John Donne, Rome, 1945.

M. P. RAMSAY. *Les Doctrines médiévales chez Donne*, Paris, 1917 (revised edn., 1924).

M. A. RUGOFF. *Donne's Imagery*, New York, 1939.

R. SENCOURT. *Outflying Philosophy*, Hildesheim, 1924.

I. SIMON. *Some Problems of Donne Criticism*. Brussels, n.d. [1952 ?].

T. SPENCER AND OTHERS. *A Garland for John Donne*, Cambridge, U.S.A., 1932.

T. SPENCER AND M. VAN DOREN. *Studies in Metaphysical Poetry*, New York, 1939.

E. M. W. TILLYARD. *The Elizabethan World Picture*, London, 1943.

R. TUVE. *Elizabethan and Metaphysical Imagery*, Chicago, 1947.

G. WILLIAMSON. *The Donne Tradition*, Cambridge, U.S.A., 1930.

B. Periodical Articles

Abbreviations for periodicals: *ELH: Journal of English Literary History; ESEA: Essays and Studies by Members of the English Association; JEGP: Journal of English and Germanic Philology; MLN: Modern Language Notes; MLR: Modern Language Review; MP: Modern Philology; PMLA: Publications of the Modern Language Association of America; PQ: Philological Quarterly; RES: Review of English Studies; SP: Studies in Philology; TLS: The Times Literary Supplement.*

The following is a selection from the great number of critical articles on Donne:

L. I. BREDVOLD. 'The Naturalism of Donne in relation to some Renaissance Traditions', *JEGP*, XXII, 1923.

J. E. V. CROFTS. 'John Donne', *ESEA*, XXII, 1937.

F. A. DOGGETT. 'Donne's Platonism', *Sewanee Review*, July–Sept. 1934.

J. B. DOUDS. 'Donne's Technique of Dissonance', *PMLA*, LII, Dec. 1937.

E. H. DUNCAN. 'Donne's Alchemical Figures', *ELH*, Dec. 1942.

G. R. ELLIOTT. 'John Donne: The Middle Phase', *Bookman*, LXXII, 1931.

H. W. GARROD. 'Donne and Mrs. Herbert', *RES*, XXI, July 1945.

D. W. HARDING. 'Coherence of Theme in Donne's Poetry', *Kenyon Review*, Summer 1951.

M. Y. HUGHES. 'The Lineage of *The Extasie*', *MLR*, XXVII, 1932.

B. JOHNSON. 'Classical Allusions in the Poetry of Donne', *PMLA*, LIII, Dec. 1938.

F. R. LEAVIS. 'The Influence of Donne on Modern Poetry', *Bookman*, March 1931.

J. LEDERER. 'John Donne and the Emblematic Practice', *RES*, XXII, July 1946.

P. LEGOUIS. 'L'état présent des controverses sur la poésie de Donne', *Études anglaises*, May 1952.

M. F. MOLONEY. 'Donne's Metrical Practice', *PMLA*, LXV, March 1950.

G. R. POTTER. 'Donne's *Extasie*, contra Legouis', *PQ*, XV, 1936.

K. RAINE: 'John Donne and the Baroque Doubt', *Horizon*, June 1945.

E. M. SIMPSON. 'A Note on Donne's Punctuation', *RES*, July 1928.

A. STEIN. 'Meter and Meaning in Donne's Verse', *Sewanee Review*, LII, 1944.

'Donne's Prosody', *PMLA*, LIX, June 1944.

'Donne's Obscurity and the Elizabethan Tradition', *ELH*, XIII, 1946.

'Structures of Sound in Donne's Verse', *Kenyon Review*, Winter and Spring 1951.

E. M. W. TILLYARD. 'A Note on Donne's *Extasie*', *RES*, Jan. 1943.

E. L. WIGGINS. 'Logic in the Poetry of John Donne', *SP*, XLII, 1945.

G. WILLIAMSON. 'The Nature of the Donne Tradition', *SP*, XXVI, 1929.
'Textual Difficulties in the Interpretation of Donne's Poetry', *MP*, XXXVIII, Aug. 1940.

M. O. WILLMORE. 'John Donne', *Quarterly Review*, June, 1930.

M. WILLY. 'The Poetry of Donne: its interest and influence today', *ESEA*, 1954.

INDEX OF FIRST LINES

INDEX OF FIRST LINES